Unions and Class Transformation

New Political Economy

RICHARD MCINTYRE, *General Editor*

Unions and Class Transformation

The Case of the Broadway Musicians

Catherine P. Mulder

Routledge
Taylor & Francis Group
New York   London

First published 2009
by Routledge
7 11 Third Ave, New York, NY 10017

Simultaneously published in the UK
by Routledge
2 Park Square, Milton Park, Abingdon, Oxon OX14 4RN

Routledge is an imprint of the Taylor & Francis Group, an informa business

First published in paperback 2012

Typeset in Sabon by IBT Global.

Library of Congress Cataloging in Publication Data
Mulder, Catherine P.
  Unions and class transformation : the case of the Broadway musicians / by Catherine P. Mulder.
    p. cm. — (New political economy)
  Includes bibliographical references and index.
  1. Musicians—Salaries, etc.—New York (State)—New York.   2. Musicians—Labor unions—New York (State)—New York.   3. Musicals—Economic aspects—New York (State)—New York.   4. American Federation of Musicians. Local 802.   I. Title.
  ML3795.M76 2008
  331.88'1178214—dc22   2008035436

ISBN13: 978-0-415-99616-7 (hbk)
ISBN13: 978-0-203-88235-1 (ebk)
ISBN13: 978-0-415-65468-5 (pbk)

For the Past, the Present and the Future.

For the past,
to my wonderful Nanny,
Catherine Butler
May 31, 1909—July 22, 2004

For the present,
to my dedicated and loving Mother,
Maureen Butler

For the future,
to my terrific nephews,
Leo Kray Jr. &
Paul Henry Kray

Contents

Figures

Tables

Acknowledgments

I thank my committee for all their comments and support, Richard Wolff, (chair), Stephen Resnick (member) and Elaine Bernard (member). I also thank the people at Routledge for publishing this book, particularly Ric McIntyre, Jennifer Morrow, Eleanor Chan, and Ben Holtzman.

There have been many family, friends, students, musicians and colleagues who have supported my research and much more through the many years.

Firstly and foremost I thank my mother, Maureen Butler whose ceaseless love and devotion, and psychological, moral and financial support is immeasurable.

I thank my sisters, Jeanne Mulder and Carol Kray, whose love and support has meant so much to me. I also thank my two terrific nephews, Leo Kray, Jr. and Paul Henry Kray; it is because of my love for them that gave me the incentive to persevere. I thank my father, Henry Mulder for his love and words of wisdom that truly inspired me. I also thank my brother-in-law, Leo Kray, my stepfather, Dominick Caccamo and my stepmother, Judith Mulder for everything they have done for me over the years.

David Brennan, my friend and colleague at Franklin & Marshall College provided me with countless hours of enthusiasm for my research; thus I thank him. It was David who got me through the laborious initial phases of this research and who was there when I had that very specific moment when the 'light bulb' went off.

Thank you to all my colleagues/friends who have been extremely supportive through out the years. Thank you to Antonio Callari, Suzanne Smith, Reshela DuPuis, Sharon Moran, Bill Mello, Brian Scott, Maria Hynson, Jody Ping, James Martin, Lisa Noetzel, Cecilia Mameli, Beth Young, Scott Pearson, and Wanda Gorman.

Without the musicians and the some staff members from Local 802, this book would not have been possible. Specifically, I would like to thank Leslie Wilkins, whose friendship and assistance is greatly acknowledged and appreciated. I would also like to thank Bill Moriarity, Seymour 'Red' Press and Ted Sperling for their candor and time in giving me interviews vital to my research.

Finally, I would like to thank all the workers in this world, because it is my dedication to workers and the labor movement that gave me the incentive for this project.

1 Unions and Class Transformation
The Case of the Broadway Musicians

A. INTRODUCTION

Trades Unions work well as centres of resistance against the encroach-ments of capital. They fail partially from an injudicious use of their power. They fail generally from limiting themselves to a guerrilla war against the effects of the existing system, instead of simultaneously try-ing to change it, instead of using their organised forces as a lever for the final emancipation of the working class, that is to say, the ultimate abolition of the wages system. (Marx, *Value* 62)

Karl Marx made the above assertion in 1865, as a rebuttal to John Weston's allegation that trade unions are harmful to industry (Marx, *Value* 5). To date, trade unions, particularly those in the United States, continue to resist "encroachments of capital" through representation and collective bargain-ing, but they make no attempt to change the existing economic system under which they labor. Many social theorists, union activists as well as union adversaries, unquestioningly accept the unions' role as representa-tive. And indeed, U.S. unions have been successful as worker represen-tatives in obtaining higher wages, more fringe benefits, and greater job security than nonunion workers have attained (AFL-CIO, "Union Differ-ence"). But these successes address only the 'effects' of capitalism, they do not address the larger picture; they fall short of advocating a change in the economic process that would include a dissolution of the social theft of the fruits of workers' labor. According to Marx:

They [unions] ought not to forget that they are fighting with effects, but not with the causes of those effects; that they are retarding the down-ward movement, but not changing its direction; that they are applying palliatives, not curing the malady. (*Value* 61)

As a result of the many failures they have encountered over the last thirty years, unions seem content to accept a very limited role as worker represen-tatives. Their lack of confidence and vision has likely exacerbated the crisis that U.S. unions currently face, and it may well compromise their position as "organized forces."

U.S. unions are in crisis. Their successes are outweighed by many set-backs, illustrated by the following statistics: between 1973 and 2000, real wages decreased approximately 10% with a simultaneous increase in labor's productivity; 44% more people are working multiple jobs (AFL-CIO, Common Sense"); and household debt per capita has increased approximately 66%.[1] Many social scientists attribute the crisis to the decreasing number of workers with union representation (Rogers; Bernstein; Rose and Chaison; McDonald; Barkin; H. Farber; Masters; Robinson; Peterson, Lee, and Finnegan; Edwards and Podgursky). As can be seen in Figure 1.1, union density rates have plummeted to 12.5% in 2004, "the lowest point in 6 decades," (US-BLS) a decline of over 56% since 1973 (Labor Research Association, Union Membership). What is more startling is that, only 7.9% of the private sector is unionized, a decline of over 70% since a 28.5% density rate in 1973 (Labor Research Association, Private Sector).

The posited causes of the decline, and the concomitant policy suggestions and union strategies, are quite diverse. For example, some of the causes include: structural shifts and attrition in organized industries (Masters; Robinson; McDonald; Barkin), globalization (Bernstein), insufficient resources

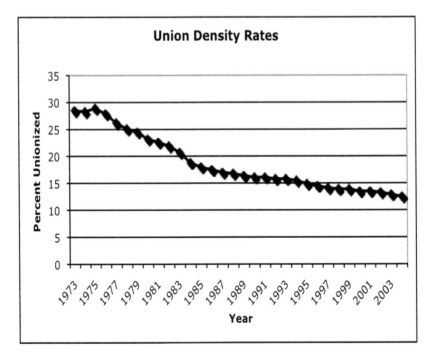

Figure 1.1 Union Density Rates. Source: Labor Research Association "Union Membership." 29 Dec. 2005 <http://www.lraonline.org/charts.php?id=29?>.

dedicated to organizing (Peterson, Lee, and Finnegan; Rose and Chaison), and employer resistance to unionization (H. Farber; Masters; Robinson; Edwards and Podgursky). A wide variety of strategies are suggested to deal with the decline: increasing efforts and resources for organizing (Barkin; H. Farber; Rose and Chaison); changing the laws, including the repeal or amendment of the National Labor Relations Act (McDonald; Peterson, Lee, and Finnegan; Masters); increasing the level of union militancy in a politically strategic manner (Robinson); union support for capitalist schemes that might increase profits (Rogers); and collective bargaining on a society-wide basis[2] (Edwards and Podgursky). What these inquiries lack is a challenge to the economic structure of capitalism. Most analysis of both the cause of and the political remedies for union decline accept the status quo and simply attempt to alter conditions within the parameters of capitalism. Since workers have been losing ground now for over 3 decades, it might be time to rethink the status quo and therefore reject capitalism for an economic structure that is more consistent with workers rights.

The analysts mentioned above are not alone in circumventing, omitting, or suppressing a critical discussion of the existing capitalist economic structure: the AFL-CIO does so as well. From its inception in the late 1800s, from Samuel Gompers to John Sweeney, the AFL-CIO has been pro-capitalist. Indeed, Gompers believed "unions must be operated like businesses to survive within capitalist society. Notions like socialist transformation were just 'pie in the sky'" (Annunziato, "Commodity" 23). American unions have not veered far from this ideology, in fact it might be argued that the unions of today are much more conservative and acquiescent to capitalists than they have ever been in the past. Of course, there have been several challenges by 'renegade' worker advocates, like the International Workers of the World (IWW), as well as subsets within particular unions like New Directions within the United Auto Workers Union. Nonetheless, these challenges while successful in opening debate, have failed in their attempts to eradicate capitalism.

What did develop was an unwritten "social compact" between labor and capital, an unwritten agreement that labor would refrain from contesting capitalism (Mantsios 52). As George Meany, the AFL-CIO's president from 1955–1979, wrote in the American Federationist, "the U.S. worker is banking on the success of the American social order . . . American workers want a fair share of the abundance they have produced . . . no more, no less" (47).[3] However, this "contract" or "pact" has been eroding since the Reagan Administration (Edwards and Podgursky). The present corporate agenda is one of union avoidance, often implemented by employing costly union-busting consulting firms[4] and attorneys. Labor's counter to the corporate agenda has rarely deviated from its traditional goal of improving the wages and working conditions of its members. The reforms advocated by unions have been quite narrow in scope, limited to such measures as the introduction of team concepts in labor/management accords.[5] Additionally, the primary opposition instrument used by labor to counter capital, the strike, was guillotined by the firing 11,000 members of the Professional Air Traffic Control Organization (PATCO) in 1981. President Reagan 'permanently' replaced all of the striking PATCO members; subsequently, private employers have behaved similarly and have 'permanently' replaced striking workers. Replacing striking workers has had a significant negative effect on the use of a strike by unions when negotiations come to a standstill. Since 1981, the incidence of strikes has significantly decreased because of the fear of union members' job losses. Figure 1.2 depicts the loss of the strike as an economic weapon against an employer (1981 is denoted by the double line).

Today's AFL-CIO espouses a "working families" agenda in which its principal strategies continue to be collective bargaining and organizing. According to the AFL-CIO:

> To counter corporate America's economic plan, workers must have their own agenda. Labor's agenda is working families' agenda; strong unions can change our economic situation!
>
> The economic struggles faced by working families are, by and large, not the result of their individual failures to work hard or make good decisions. Their problems are not personal ones—they are part of a national pattern that can be addressed *only* through organizing and

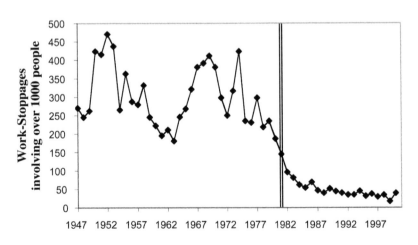

Post World War II Work Stoppages

Figure 1.2 Post World War II Work Stoppages. US Bureau of Labor Statistics. 25 Jan. 2006 <http://146.142.4.24/cgi-bin/surveymost?ws>.

collective action. Through our unions, we must fight for our economic security. It's up to us! ("Unions and the Economy")

By its own standard of success, increasing union density rates, the AFL-CIO falls short.

This book provides an alternative to the "social compact" that has clearly failed workers in the United States by examining a specific group of workers, i.e., the Broadway musicians. Unions and their analysts might initiate—or reopen—a debate that challenges the existing economic structure, thereby calling into question the existing class positions workers now hold and propose a work environment that is more consistent with workers' values and one that is not morally abhorrent. In other words, it is time to rethink traditional analyses and to propose a new and innovative agenda, which includes the possibility for class transformation (economic revolution) and utilizes unions and their many resources as agents of change.

The traditional/orthodox literature impedes such a debate and/or analysis; therefore, I have chosen the radical and novel theoretical approach of New Marxian Class Analysis (NMCA) which provides the researcher with the tools necessary to understand and, therefore, suggest changes to improve the lives of working people, something other more traditional theoretical approaches do not (Resnick and Wolff, 1987). NMCA also provides the researcher with a technique to suggest possible transformation of the economic structure of particular workers. As will be discussed below, the Broadway musicians are one such group of workers who might witness an improvement in their working lives, which would not necessarily occur without the analysis provided in this book.

B. NEW MARXIAN CLASS ANALYSIS

In the Marxian tradition, a class-transformative/revolutionary agenda is one that promotes a change from the current mode of production to another, such as a change from the capitalist class process to the communist class process will be developed in this book. Such a shift has the intention of improving the working conditions of workers. Using the analytical techniques provided by NMCA I demonstrate that a transformation from a capitalist class process to one of communism is not only desirable but also feasible, despite the prevailing economic, political, and cultural circumstances. That is, this book will negate the "pie in the sky" standpoint of Samuel Gompers as well as other union advocate commentators.

In the NMCA framework, "[c]lass is understood as a distinct social process . . . [I]t is the economic process of performing and appropriating surplus labor" (Resnick and Wolff, *Knowledge* 26). Surplus labor is the labor performed that exceeds the necessary labor workers executes "to produce the consumables customarily required by the direct producer to keep working" (115). Workers in capitalism, for example, receive wages for their necessary labor, yet they receive no payments for surplus labor they perform; the capitalists appropriate their entire surplus. To be sure, surplus is produced in every mode of production; however, the operative class process is revealed only when one determines who appropriates—and thus distributes—the surplus. Within capitalism, someone other than its direct producer appropriates the surplus, and this process is known as exploitation. Surplus that is "appropriated directly and immediately by nonlaborers . . . is Marx's precise definition of exploitation" (20). This appropriator, or more often these appropriators are themselves the capitalists and the committers of worker exploitation. A preferable class process is one devoid of exploitation, one in which the surplus is appropriated by its producers, such as communism. In a communist class process, the laborers themselves, collectively, directly, and immediately appropriate any surplus they produce. In communism, there is no social theft of the surplus produced by the workers as there exists within capitalism.

> If one rejects collective appropriation, one also rejects the right of individuals to participate on an equal footing in making decisions concerning issues that are of central importance to their lives and that affect the better part of their waking hours. (Cullenberg 78)

A communist class process is preferable to that of a capitalist class process, firstly because within capitalism workers toil a certain portion of their workday for which they are not compensated for that work.[6] That is, while the capitalist must pay the workers a specific wage for his/her necessary labor, any surplus produced by the workers is summarily taken by the capitalist. Thus, the stealing of the surplus by capitalists is morally and ethically reprehensible because it is exploitative; therefore a communist class structure is preferred. Secondly, a communist class structure may make it possible for workers to make improvements in their own working lives. As stated above, workers in a communist class structure appropriate the surplus they produce; therefore, the workers themselves might not only make surplus distributions in ways that will secure their conditions of existence as communist workers, but may also make surplus distributions to improve their lives. Finally, a communist class process is preferred over capitalism because it might allow the workers to democratically participate in their own working lives. Democracy has been championed in the political arena, but it has yet to become part of the integral fabric of the workplace. Acting as worker representatives, unions can use their many financial and collective resources to facilitate a class transformation from capitalism to communism. In this way, they can increase the likelihood that the workers' goals—both class and non-class—will be achieved.

In a communist class structure, democracy is not a given, however, unions can ensure democratic allocation of the workers' surplus to institutions, laws, and social structures, and this may result in a work/social environment that is more amenable to workers and their communities. In a communist situation, workers could make surplus distributions that support worker-friendly institutions, laws, and social structures. That is, workers will spend their surplus to benefit themselves. For example, surplus distributions could be made to support politicians who profess to have the workers' best interests as one of their primary issues. Conversely, workers could withhold surplus distributions that sustain a capitalist class process, thus possibly undermining and compromising its continued existence. Consequently, the best interests of workers and their communities might be better served if they employed alternative means such as withholding surplus distributions from political parties that support 'big business' or promote international trade without accountability. They might also withhold distributions from businesses that use environmentally destructive technologies, while making distributions to firms that advocate and utilize environmentally sustainable technologies so that workers and their families will have a future that is not compromised by capitalist decisions that are based solely on profit maximization. To be sure, workplace improvements in a communist class process are not inevitable, nor are there any guarantees of success; however, the probability of success should increase when those who are affected by the outcome are involved in the decision-making processes regarding the appropriation and distribution of the surplus. Yet because union analysts do not look at class issues in terms of surplus labor, it is highly unlikely that a class-transformative agenda, a central component of NMCA, will be forthcoming. Marx " . . . sought to remedy the failure of other analysts, and especially of the social critics and radicals he saw as his allies, to understand the capitalist class structure and to include its transformation explicitly on their agendas for social change" (Wolff 116).

Marx wrote that unions should have a dual agenda: not only should they strive to improve workers' circumstances within capitalism, but they should also strive to abolish capitalism itself. Only when the latter goal is achieved will workers obtain a work environment in which they have a true voice in their working lives. A communist class process also yields non-class[7] social changes that workers desire such as better public education and worker training. Ergo, a transformation of the class structure will not only have direct effects on the workers themselves, but could potentially have more far reaching outcomes.

Workers in a communist class process could make surplus distributions that would improve their lives both internal and external to their work. Communist workers, for example, might alter the internal political process of supervisory duties. Communist workers could acquire the process of supervisory power once wielded by capitalists or their agents, achieving greater worker control over the production process and a greater sense of worker pride and self-worth. Furthermore, natural processes might be improved upon by communist workers' consumption and production surplus distribution decisions.

Workers in a communist class process might produce and consume goods and services that are reliable, nontoxic, and harmless. They may also choose to support sustainable, environmentally friendly technologies without the fear of losing their jobs. Communist workers may also choose to modify some of the cultural standards promoted by capitalists and their agents. For example, communist workers might choose to support increased leisure time so that they could enjoy more of the arts, time with their families, or time to participate in community and political affairs. Additionally, communist workers could choose to disseminate and promote healthy lifestyles, encouraging exercise and a nutritious diet, for example, while simultaneously discouraging unhealthy behaviors like cigarette smoking and other addictions that have been a staple of capitalism for the last two hundred years. Communist workers might also make changes in economic processes in that they might support and make available credit instruments with more favorable terms than the ones that are currently in effect. That is not to say that mortgages and other types of consumer loans would be interest-free, but workers might choose to decrease the profit margin from the current levels. Communist workers could also support education and training of young people so that they might retire earlier than workers currently do, and they might simultaneously support reasonable pension programs that offer workers a truly sustainable retirement lifestyle. They could support and defend their own job security and support retraining programs when technological advances are made. Finally, workers might increase their payments for work rendered, increasing their real as well as their relative wages by making decisions that support whatever they think will accomplish their agenda. The point is, workers could make decisions that prioritize their own well being, rather than prioritizing the maximization of profits as capitalists do, which only increases the well-being of a few. These are possible outcomes of a discourse that focuses on, or at least includes, a discussion of class-transformation.[8] Of course, there are no guarantees of positive outcomes, however, just including these goals in a worker-focused agenda could be beneficial to the workers and their communities.

Most union discourses, however, endeavor to improve workers' conditions within a capitalist class structure; they do not have a class-transformative agenda, nor do they even consider one. This, according to Marx, is a "failure" of unions. The discourses in economic democracy, which are usually limited to issues such as worker cooperatives and employee participation schemes, allude to transformation, yet their lack of focus on surplus value issues serves to inhibit class transformation. The primary common tenet of these theoretical constructs is that those who do the work should have a "voice" in the work process; it is "voice" that is the essence of these theoretical approaches (Hirschman, 1970). Scholars, workers, and unions alike have no general agreement on how much "voice" the workers should have and how "voice" should be defined. Some authors see a role for unions in facilitating change in the work process and advocate more worker participation and/or autonomy (Bernard; Yates; Maranto), while others view democratic work sites as a possible alternative to unions (Freeman and Rogers), and still others disregard unions entirely (Ellerman). NMCA offers an alternative to the present literature, and using the NMCA theoretical approach could allow for either a complete overhaul of capitalism; or, possibly, a more modest proposal that retains capitalism, but in a form that gives workers more input in their work lives than they do in the existing economic structure. As Resnick and Wolff state:

> A radical shift from a highly structured system of authority and command to a more egalitarian structure in which power to command is democratized and shared within the enterprise can be quite consistent with a changed but still existing capitalist appropriation of surplus value. (*Knowledge* 168)

The addition surplus appropriation and distribution into the economic democracy literature could yield a more fruitful discussion and therefore alter the way capitalism is perceived.

As worker advocates, unions with their collective forces and their many resources have the opportunity to be the agents of social change and class transformation. By using NMCA a specific case study of a particular group of union workers can demonstrate how transformation becomes a possibility. A case study focusing on the issue of surplus will highlight the differences between capitalists and workers and thus contradict much of the current worker advocate literature, which claims that a cohesive team effort is advantageous for all parties (Rogers; Ellerman; Applebaum and Batt). Furthermore, a case study can also demonstrate how unions may themselves inhibit class transformation and increased workplace democracy. For example, unions typically oppose dismantling or even amending the National Labor Relations Act (McDonald; Peterson, Lee, and Finnegan; Masters). The act itself makes it difficult for union members to function as surplus appropriators, since the act prohibits union workers from acting in a supervisory capacity. A case study using NMCA may also reveal methods to improve existing working conditions, increase union membership, and enhance the social standing of unions in the United States. This book analyzes a specific group of union workers, the Broadway musicians, using the NMCA framework to illustrate how their current agenda and strategies may be responsible for many of the problems they encounter. Therefore, a prototype of a class-transformative agenda is offered, and a subsequent discussion of its feasibility.

C. NMCA AND THE BROADWAY MUSICIANS: AN OVERVIEW

In the chapters that follow, the theoretical approach of NMCA will be applied to a specific group of workers, namely the Broadway musicians. The

Broadway musicians are an interesting group of workers to investigate in that their circumstances, personal and professional, are unlike many other union workers; however, at the same time, they endure many of the issues and problems workers in other industries are forced to tolerate. Unlike workers in other industries, the Broadway musicians enjoy a 100% union density rate, yet like other industrial workers suffer from health and safety issues that can be detrimental to their health and future employment. While highly skilled, educated, experienced, and trained, the Broadway musicians have relatively little job security, which is a primary benefit to union workers in other industries. The similarities and differences to other unionized workers will become evident in the chapters below. Then, the final chapter will show how the Broadway musicians and possibly other union workers could improve their situations, both professional and personal, via a class transformation that is provided using the theoretical approach of NMCA.

Of course simply focusing on a single case study comes with some limitations such as its applicability to other union workers, particular those in industrial unions. That is, unlike typical craft unions, union workers in industrial setting often have a variety of different work assignments, skills, experience and education. The analysis and subsequent suggestions presented here might at first glance not seem relevant in an industrial setting, however, the with some modifications and adaptations, one might visualize its extension. Additionally, with a detailed focus on a specific group of workers allows for the reader to obtain an appreciation of the intricacies of any work environment.

A detailed description of the Broadway musicians and the agents with whom they contend with daily is provided in Chapter 2. The discussion commences with an introduction to the industry of Broadway musicals. This is necessary because of the uniqueness of the industry; it is simultaneously a capitalist for profit industry and an integral part of New York's City's cultural landscape and a tourist destination. A subsequent explanation of capitalism's existence on Broadway, which is often veiled by the notion of collective creativity of the Broadway participants, will reveal that capitalism is indeed the reigning class structure in existence on Broadway. An investigation of the typical legal structure of a Broadway show will explain that the Producers[9] of the Broadway musicals are the capitalists. Once capitalism and the capitalist class positions on Broadway are identified, a discussion will follow regarding the various agents who ensure conditions of existence the Producer's qua capitalist's position.

Chapter 2 also includes a complete investigation of the Broadway musicians and the specific conditions in which they toil. Their wages and working conditions indicate that improvements can and should be made. While the Broadway musicians enjoy many more advantages that other union workers are denied, they remain exploited capitalist workers and, therefore, endure the consequences of such positions. This discussion is followed by a synopsis of the Broadway musicians' foreman, the conductor. This position, as will be seen below, is one of severe contradictions. What follows is the very interesting position that the Music Coordinator (MC) possesses in the production of a Broadway musical.

Finally, Chapter 2 concludes with a summary of the Broadway musicians' union, The Associated Musicians of Greater New York, Local 802 of the American Federation of Musicians (Local 802). It will be made clear in this section that Local 802, while striving for the best wages and working conditions it can achieve for the Broadway musicians, simultaneously reinforces some of the issues and problems the musician endure because it does not challenge the capitalist structure on Broadway.

The Broadway musicians experience a variety of problems that workers in other industries face, but they also endure problems that are unique to the theatrical industry. In Chapter 3 there is a comprehensive examination of the concerns of the Broadway musicians such as safety and health issues involving special effects, amplified music, and repetitive stress disorders. While Local 802 has addressed these problems in recent collective bargaining agreements, complete elimination of the health hazards has not come to fruition.

Chapter 3 also includes a discussion of the lack of worker participation, i.e. 'voice' and job security. The musicians, unlike other union workers, but like non-union workers, do not have a significant amount of worker participation or job security on Broadway. The Broadway musicians' job security is also threatened by the increased reliance on electronic instrumentation by the Producers. Virtual Orchestra's (VOs) have been invented and have been used as a threat to the Broadway musicians, to replace them if they should strike.

Because of these and other concerns that the Broadway musicians face and endure, a class transformative prototype is provided in Chapter 4. This prototype demonstrates that the Broadway musicians would change the class structure under which they toil, allowing a transformation of the existing capitalist process on Broadway into a new communist process for the musicians. With the assistance of Local 802, the musicians would simply form their own orchestras. The Broadway musicians would then sell the commodity music to the Producers, rather than selling their labor power, an exploitative position, as they do now. By transforming the class structure, the musicians might not endure many, if any of the concerns addressed in Chapter 3. Furthermore, the musicians may make improvements in their professional as well as their personal lives by having the freedom from the threat of job loss due to the now redundant position of the MC. This and other benefits of class-transformation will be detailed in Chapter 4.

Furthermore, Chapter 4 includes a discussion regarding the working conditions in a post class transformation arena. The Broadway musicians and Local 802 will have not only different benefits, but will also be burdened with additional responsibilities. For example, the musicians will have to develop a process by which orchestra members are hired. The hiring process proposed is based on a democratic process. Local 802 would have the added responsibility of ensuring that the musicians adhere to hiring standards.

Chapter 4 also includes the post transformative relationships the musicians will have with the other Broadway participants, including the Producers, the Music Coordinators, the Theatre owners, the Broadway League (hereafter, the League), and the conductors. For example, Local 802 would also have the responsibility of negotiating contracts with the capitalist Producers. Furthermore, in a post transformation situation, the role of the Music Coordinator would now be redundant; thus there might be a complete elimination of the position. The elimination of the MC would also give the musicians the opportunity to actively engage in the work process and have 'voice' without retaliation. This as well as other post transformation relationships will be detailed in Chapter 4.

Chapter 5, the concluding chapter, will include an account of how the musicians concerns address in Chapter 3, might be eliminated or reduced in a post transformative situation. A complete discussion of changes in safety and health, worker participation, and job security will be provided in the concluding chapter. Also, Chapter 5 will include a discussion on the possibility for other workers, whether union or not, to develop their own class transformative agenda. This book should serve as a template for unions to follow in their efforts to improve the circumstances of their members.

Using the NMCA allows one to restructure and rethink the work relationship to exclude or eliminate exploitation entirely. That is the goal of this book: to provide the reader with an alternative agenda that to date has not been attempted by most unions. Exploitation elimination, as will be shown in the chapters to follow, could have serious positive consequences for workers, and also new responsibilities. However, in an arena sans exploitation workers will have more control over their own destiny by the choices and payments from the surplus they make.

While the changes proposed here might not seem very radical or revolutionary because only one group of workers will be affected, if implemented on a larger scale, or by multiple unions, the current assault on workers in industrialized nations might be reversed. That is, workers in industrialized nations are currently witnessing their jobs being outsourced, downsized, or transferred to less developed nations where wages are less than theirs. Because of this, workers in many industries are experiencing losses of bargaining power, decreases in their real wages, and elimination and/or reduction in their benefits (Gapasin and Yates 3). If workers in these industries adopted a class transformative agenda, they might be able to reverse this trend and witness improving rather deteriorating working conditions. While the work here may only be a modest attempt at improving the professional lives of the Broadway musicians, there is the possibility for expansion to other workers. In the chapters that follow, the reader will be provided with a clear understanding of the musicians, their working environment, and the possibility of improving their circumstances. Moreover, a template is provided so that other workers might use the analysis and prototype to make changes in other circumstances.

2   The Broadway Musicians
A Case Study

A. INTRODUCTION

New York City has a private sector unionization rate of only 14.6% (Labor Research Association, "Unions Have Resources"); however, the Broadway Theatre is a 'union' industry. Virtually every one of the 75,000 Broadway employees belongs to a union, even workers with supervisory duties belong to unions, and if Broadway workers are not in an 'official' union, then they are part of a guild or another type of collective centered on their mutual interests.

> Every group except the authors has a union. Stagehands have a union. Directors have a guild. Writers have a guild in name, but it's not a union. It's the only group that cannot legally bargain in the theater today because of anti-trust action brought against it decades ago. (Rosenberg and Harburg 22)

Most theatrical workers belong to one of 13 trade unions; these unions include the Actors' Equity Association (AEA); Society of Stage Directors and Choreographers (SSD&C); Theatrical Protective Union Stage Hands, Local 1 (IATSE); and the primary focus of this project, the Associated Musicians of Greater New York, Local 802, AFM (hereafter, Local 802). In addition, what makes Broadway especially interesting is that even the employers belong to their own collective, the Broadway League. Like trade unions, the League acts as the sole-bargaining agent for most Broadway employers, but the relationship between the various Broadway agents is simultaneously unique and conventional. While the Broadway theatre industry has some peculiar traits that make it an interesting research endeavor, it is at the same time a capitalist profit-maximizing industry.

In capitalist industries with high union density rates, workers tend to enjoy more worker control over their working conditions, more benefits, and higher wages than their non-union counterparts. Moreover, worker turnover is more infrequent in union shops. While Broadway workers realize many of the gains from unionization like other union workers, they are exploited workers as in any capitalist enterprise and thus do not participate in surplus decisions that might affect their working lives. Even with a 100% unionization rate, Broadway workers, particularly the actors and the musicians, have very little, if any, long-run job security; this is due to the fact that Broadway shows close within a relatively short time. For example the longest running Broadway musical was opened for 17 years; however, most shows close within six months of their opening nights. Broadway workers have some job security on a per show basis, but they are not assured constant or any work after the show closes.

This chapter begins with a brief introduction about Broadway's longstanding contribution to New York City's economy to be followed by investigation of the legal structure of the enterprise. Next there is a complete account of the agents directly associated with Broadway musicians, namely the theater owners, the League, the musicians themselves, the conductors, the union, and the music coordinators (MC). Understanding the various participants and their positions within the capitalist structure and their intricate relationships with the musicians reveals the issues the musicians confront may be exacerbated, or remain unchanged. Moreover, knowledge of the participants' roles and responsibilities will expose areas where progressive class-transformative changes can be made.

B. BROADWAY, THE INDUSTRY

Live musical theatre on Broadway has been a major New York City tourist attraction, institution, and industry since the 18th century. The New York theatre industry has survived wars, depressions, and technological changes. Its longevity is inexplicable given that undertaking a Broadway musical is a very precarious financial investment in that each season between 70 and 80 percent result in losses to their investors (D. Farber, 89 *Producing Theatre*; Rosenberg 14). Nonetheless, Broadway theatre remains a vital New York City industry, with box-office revenues exceeding $769 million in the 2004–2005 season alone. During the 2000–2001 season, Broadway witnessed the highest ticket prices on record and Producers queued for vacant theatres (McKinley, "On Stage and Off"). Broadway supports 40,000 jobs (League, *Broadway's Economic Contribution* 26) and over 1600 ancillary businesses (Labor Research Association, "Unions Have Resources" 3). Broadway's relative importance in the New York economy, particularly in the tourism industry, became quite evident during the 2003 musicians' strike due to the media's attention, the overall sense of economic emergency, and Mayor Michael Bloomberg's fervent attempts to settle the strike.

The Broadway theatre industry is "the single largest tourist attraction in New York City" (Labor Research Association, "Unions Have Resources" 3). According to a report by the League of American Theatres and Producers, "nearly 12 million people attended Broadway shows during the 2000–2001 season" (League, *Broadway's Economic Contribution* 6), and its economic contribution to New York City that season was estimated at $4.42 billion (5); this represents a real increase of 50% from the 1998–1999 season (28). Furthermore, while audiences paid almost $2 billion directly to the Broadway industry, their indirect expenditures amounted to another $893.6 million (13). Approximately 56% of the audience spending comes from tourists, 47% from U.S. visitors and 9.3% from international visitors. The industry, however, continues to draw 43.8% of its audiences from the New York metropolitan area: 24.4% from the suburbs and 19.4% from New York City boroughs (League, *Broadway's Economic Contribution* 7). Furthermore, "[e]xcluding corporate profit taxes, an estimated $139 million in local tax revenues may be traced directly to the Broadway industry" (25).

Much of Broadway's economic contribution comes directly from expenses of the production itself. It has been estimated that Broadway companies expenses on "payroll, supplies, and services to produce and run shows added $1.5 billion to the city's economy" (League, *Broadway's Economic Contribution* 14). Broadway operating costs for the 2000–2001 season totaled $546.3 million (18), a 72.5% increase from the1991–1992 season (20). On average, salaries and fixed royalties[1] accounted for more than 50% of the operating costs of a musical (19). The expenses associated with the production of a Broadway musical are indeed considerable; nonetheless the expenses themselves have a direct positive effect on New York City's economic viability.

One would expect Broadway, like most other labor-intensive service industries, to have significant labor expenditures, but this is not the case. For most US firms, labor accounts for 60% of production costs, an estimate that includes both goods and services; therefore, Broadway labor costs are below the national average at 50% (Economic Policy Institute). There has often been much discussion and controversy over the ostensibly 'exorbitant' labor costs, particularly during contract negotiations with the various Broadway unions. These claims are made by the Producers and Theatre Owners and are simply employed to 'shock' the public and shed blame on the workers for the relatively high-ticket prices. Subterfuges like this, however, are typical in any capitalist industry; workers and their 'high' wages are targeted as the primary reason for high or increasing prices of goods or services. As will be discussed below, the Broadway theatre is capitalist, and therefore the Producers respond as typical capitalists with their primary agenda being profit maximization.

C. CAPITALISM ON BROADWAY

In an "acquisitive society," art, like every other organized activity, has its economic manifestations; and of all the arts none is more firmly tied to its economic moorings than is the theatre ... The theatre emerges when dramatic literature is enacted by players on a stage before an audience. It is this transfiguration from literature to production that involves

large outlays of money and requires a complex, organized business ma-
chinery. (Bernheim 2)

There is little argument about Broadway's contribution to the economic
viability of New York City, especially its notable role in the tourism
industry. What is not obvious, however, is that Broadway has a capitalist
structure. There is an erroneous belief by many of the Broadway participants, including the Producers themselves, that capitalism, until recently,
was non-existent on Broadway and that somehow Broadway operates
outside of capitalism (McKinley). Actually, Broadway is a collective of
creative people who organize their various talents and thereby construct
an elaborate musical extravaganza in a capitalist industry. In its organizational structure, Broadway is a complex amalgamated industry that
organizes many participants, each with his/her unique contribution, for
the production of a Broadway musical; much like any other capitalist
enterprise. Nonetheless, even scholars of American theatre continuously
reinforce the non-recognition of capitalism on Broadway. For example,
Arvid Sponberg writes, "[a]n irony of theater history lies in this: Theater
may be a collaborative art—even a communal art—but it is experienced
individually" (xv). Conversely, it is obvious to those in the 'business of
Broadway' that it is indeed a for-profit industry, and that the collaboration process is similar to one in almost any capitalist industry. Yet,
on Broadway, the idea of it as a profit-maximizing capitalist institution
has been historically repugnant, particularly to creative groups. This is
not the case, however, for the Producers and theatre owners; they are
unapologetic for being profit seekers. No matter what the appearance,
capitalism is unmistakable on Broadway.

The illusion of cooperation, collaboration, or communalism is not unique
to Broadway. Indeed, Marx's fundamental mission was to expose the atroc-
ities of capitalism and its inherent exploitation of capitalist workers that is
veiled by the notion of cooperation in the capitalist mode of production.
Marx, in Volume I of *Capital*, provided a sophisticated discussion about
how cooperation by the workers in capitalist enterprises is a condition of
existence of capitalism. Marx's notion of cooperation is as such:

> When numerous workers work together side by side in accordance with
> a plan, whether is the same process, or in different but connected pro-
> cesses, this form of labour is called co-operation. (443)

Cooperation in this instance is for the benefit of the capitalist who assembles the workers, so that s/he can reap the rewards, i.e., the surplus, from
the workers' so-called cooperation. Marx states:

> Moreover, the co-operation of wage-labourers is entirely brought about
> by the capital that employs them. Their unification into one single

productive body, and the establishment of a connection between their individual functions, lies outside their competence. (*Capital vol. 1* 449)

The relationship between capital and labor, which from the outside looks as if there is cooperation amongst the participants, is indeed antagonistic (450). The Broadway musical is no exception; the difference between Broadway and other capitalist enterprises lies only in the perception of the workers, employers, and the audience. Somehow, when creative endeavors are undertaken, the veil of capitalism is more opaque than, for example, in a manufacturing plant. When one hears a discussion about an artistic endeavor, s/he hears terms like 'creative team' among others, and s/he is led to believe that there is a group of people who collaborate on the production of such an endeavor. But this is true in many enterprises.

Historically, however erroneous, there has been a sense of collaboration on Broadway, and the Producers and workers alike reinforce it. Such deceptive implications notwithstanding, Broadway is like any other capitalist industries in that its primary objective is profit maximization. Workers in most capitalist industries cooperate with each other in one form or the other; but the theatrical community has the illusion that somehow it is different because of the artistic and creative talents associated with any theatrical production. From the 1930s to the 1980s, a duopoly of two firms dominated Broadway: the Nederlander and the Shubert Organizations. By the 1980s another firm, Jujamcyn Theatres managed to seize a portion of the industry, thereby forming a formidable oligopoly (Rosenberg 5). Until recently these three firms owned every Broadway theatre. Moreover, they were also the Producers for many Broadway productions. Since the late 1980s the industry has expanded to include more national and international entrepreneurs; nevertheless, Nederlander, Shubert, and Jujamcyn remain imposing. By 1997, the oligopoly was threatened by the purchase and restoration of two Broadway theatres by large corporations. In 1997, the Buena Vista Theatrical Corporation, a division of the Walt Disney Corporation, opened the New Amsterdam theatre; and in 1998, Livent restored and opened the Ford Center for the Performing Arts. After Livent declared bankruptcy, the mega-entertainment firm, Clear Channel purchased the Ford Center. These two corporations represent a relatively small portion of the Broadway theatres and productions but have significantly impacted the industry by exercising or merely threatening their financial might.

Capitalism, or at least the forthright discussion of Broadway capitalism, was veiled until Disney opened its first Broadway production, "Beauty and the Beast," in 1994. Subsequently, there was much furor about avaricious profit-making Broadway capitalists and how Disney reshaped the economic structure of the Broadway industry (McKinley, "Having Reshaped Broadway"). This is erroneous. The difference between large corporations like Disney and Clear Channel and that of the other Broadway capitalists is simply a legal distinction. That is, Disney and Clear Channel are publicly traded stock corporations, whereas most of the other Producers are not. [2] A specific distinction among enterprise structures that is relative to Broadway is the fact that Disney and Clear Channel do not necessarily require specific investors for each production like the other Broadway firms do. Disney currently has three musicals open on Broadway, "Beauty and the Beast," "Aida," and the "Lion King," and it owns but one of the 32 Broadway theatres. Clear Channel only has one open production, "42nd Street," and like Disney, it only owns one theatre. In spite of this, simply because of their relative size, popularity, and financial resources, Disney and Clear Channel's influence and relative impact on Broadway have increased over the last 10 years.

Like any capitalist enterprise, the Broadway musical has complexities that must be made palpable for this investigation. Conversely, and unlike other capitalist enterprises, it is not immediately obvious that, firstly, a Broadway enterprise is indeed capitalist and, secondly, the very identity of the capitalist is surreptitious in Broadway theatre. In the discussion that follows, the various positions of the agents involved in a Broadway enterprise will be elucidated and explained so that the reader will have an unambiguous comprehension of how Broadway theatre is organized. As previously noted, the positions discussed will be limited only to those who have a direct impact on the class position(s) of the musicians. This is not to say that those workers who are absent from the analysis are any less important to the enterprise. For example, absent from the discussion to follow are actors and stagehands; however, one could hardly make an argument that these positions are somehow less important than the musicians. On the contrary, Bill Moriarity, Past President of Local 802, stated that had it not been for actors' and stagehands' solidarity by refusing to cross the musicians' picket line during the 2003 strike, the strike would have been a complete failure (Moriarity, Interview). As was explained in the previous chapter, the crucial criterion for an enterprise to be deemed capitalist is that the people who produce the surplus labor are not those who appropriate it; therefore, the necessary next step in this project is to uncover who exactly the capitalist is and what his/her relationship to the surplus value producers is. On Broadway, as will become evident below, the Producers appropriate the surplus produced by the musicians.[3] And to secure their position as capitalists, Producers must make payments to various agents including theatre owners, conductors, the League, and the workers. An explanation of the various positions, structure, and responsibilities of the capitalist participants vis-à-vis the musicians follows in this chapter. The contextual NMCA class analysis, however, will be deferred until Chapter 4, where it will be presented with a class-transformative alternative structure.

1. The Capitalist: The Producer

> Who then is the boss in a theoretically "democratic family," or com-
> munity where every member sees himself as a collaborator contractu-
> ally bound to all the others? The [theatrical] lawyer [Donald] Farber's
> spontaneous answer to this question is categorical: "The producer is
> the boss. Why? Because he hires and fires. Only the producer can run
> the show." Not the director? "But the producer hires the director." No
> paradox about this. (Rosenberg and Harburg 230–1)

Being the 'boss' who has the license to hire and fire does not in itself make
the Producer the capitalist. Hiring and firing privileges might be a condition of existence for the capitalist, but it is not sufficient within a NMCA
framework. The capitalist is the appropriator and thus distributor of surplus value that s/he does not produce him/herself. In *Capital Volume
III*, Marx clearly delimits the capitalist "as one who only exploits labor"
(Resnick and Wolff, *Knowledge* 206). However, in this instance, theatrical attorney Donald Farber's implication that the Producer is the boss is
absolutely accurate, and the boss, in this case, is indeed the capitalist.
To understand the capitalist structure of a Broadway enterprise, it is first
necessary to discuss its legal formation, which will enable the reader
to understand where and how a class-transformative agenda might be
achievable.

A. Legal Structure of Broadway Musicals

For approximately the 70 years prior to 1995, the typical legal structure
of most Broadway Producers was the 'limited partnership.' This arrangement was preferred to corporate structure because of the tax advantages
it provided. Profits from limited partnerships are not subject to double
taxation policies that corporations face: corporations pay taxes once
as revenue and then again as corporate profits (D. Farber, *Producing
Theatre* 60–61). Nevertheless, limited partnerships are not without their
own set of problems in that the partners assume personal financial lia-
bilities. Thus, when the new enterprise structure of the Limited Liability
Company (LLC) was enacted by the New York State legislature in 1995,
the limited partnership formation became passé on Broadway. Now, the
LLC is the Broadway Producers'[4] structure of choice because it has the
"tax advantages of a partnership and the freedom from liability for the
principals of the company" (D. Farber, *Producing Theatre* 60). Specifically, an LLC provides protection from personal liability to its members,
the Producer and the investors, without the tax disadvantages of a corporation. It is a mélange of the more attractive aspects of a limited partnership and a corporation.

Prior to acquiring a musical, the producing company (the Producer), whether an individual or, more likely, a group of individuals, legally forms an LLC and then secures investors.[5] Next, the Producer obtains a 'property' from the book writer(s), composer(s), and lyrist(s). A theatre is subsequently leased. After that, the director, the choreographers, the music director, the music coordinator and other personnel are employed. Finally, actors, stagehands, musicians, and the remainder of the staff are hired. Ultimately, however, the Producer initiates this chain-reaction of employment and investment by forming the LLC for the production of a Broadway musical. In return for setting the Production in motion, the Producer is the first recipient of the gross box office receipts, in other words, the Producer is the first recipient of the surplus. From that surplus, s/he makes distributions that s/he is culturally or legally obliged. These social processes of forming a LLC and the subsequent organization of the workers and means of production and the fact that the Producer is the first recipient of the surplus specifically identifies the Producer as the Broadway capitalist.

Not only are the Producers the first recipient of the surplus value, they are also the first recipients of the "gross profits" which might increase further the amount of surplus value they keep for themselves. From the gross profits most LLC agreements include provisions that the Producers make payments to various entities, that is they are legally bound to make payments to certain individuals or institutions that secure their positions as Broadway capitalists. For example, most LLC agreements include the provision that Producers must make payments to investors so that investors may recover their initial outlays. These payments, however are only required once the first "net"[6] profits are realized.[7] The legal definition of "net" profits is:

> [T]he excess of Gross Receipts over all Production Expenses, Running Expenses, and other Expenses. This shall include any Production Expenses incurred or paid out by the Managing Member[8] prior to the inception of the Company [LLC], for which the Managing member shall be reimbursed upon Total Capitalization. (D. Farber, *Producing Theatre* 436)

When the initial investment is realized, the Producers and the investors (in proportion to their investment) equally share any future "net" profits. The Producer receives 50% and the investors share the other 50% (62).[9] These expenses[10] consist of salaries (including the Producer's), payroll taxes and benefits, fixed royalties, rentals (theatre, props, electrics, sound), advertising/publicity costs, and general and administrative costs including the office manager fee, insurance, legal, accounting, and office expenditures (League, *Broadway's Economic Contribution* 19). In the 2000–2001, the "total direct expenses (production and weekly running costs) of Broadway shows totaled an estimated $657.6 million (20),[11] however, only $666.2 million in 'gross receipts' were reported in the same season, thus making the claim that profits for the 2000–2001 season were only $8.6 million for all 28 Broadway productions" ("Broadway Season"). These accounting and legally bound payments secure the Producer's position as capitalist.

B. The Capitalist also known as the "Managing Member"

Because of the described political and cultural processes, the managing member qua Producer is legally and culturally understood to be in full control of the entire Production. Because s/he is also the person who initially receives all the receipts of the musical, s/he is in the position to first distribute those receipts. It follows that the Broadway Producer[12] is the 'managing member' of the LLC. S/he signs LLC operating agreement with investors and other Broadway principals. The duties, rights, and responsibilities are clearly demarcated in the LLC operating agreement and by New York state law. Specifically, and as will become apparent in the subsequent discussion, what is critical to this analysis is the fact that "the managing member has the right to make all of the decisions for the company, and is—and should be—responsible as decision maker" (D. Farber, *Producing Theatre* 63). The managing member is reimbursed for all his/her expenditures in forming the operating agreement, including but not limited to "attorneys' fees, accountants' fees, script duplication costs, and similar expenses" (64). The managing member receives the gross box office receipts[13] and has the sole responsibility of distributing those receipts to the various claimants. As stated in the LLC's operating agreement: "[t]he Managing Member shall have the absolute right to establish, as the amount thereof, such sums[14] as he, in his sole discretion, shall deem advisable" (435). The term of an LLC commences with the filing of the operating agreement with the New York Secretary of State and terminates on a specified date at which time the managing member must liquidate all assets (64).

The managing member controls the entire production, including the distribution of payments to various participants (investors, employees, and playwrights) and a "Producer's" fee for his/her services, typically one to two percent of the gross weekly box office receipts (D. Farber, *Producing Theatre* 68). What this indicates is that the managing member receives a distribution from the musical, even if the Production is not profitable. S/he also makes a payment to him/herself for office facilities that are used for the production, including secretarial services, telephones, office space and supplies. This payment is deemed a "cash office charge" and typically ranges between $1000 and $3000 for a Broadway show (D. Farber, *Producing Theatre* 68). The "managing member has complete control of production of the play and the exploitation of all rights in the play. The investor members have no rights to make decisions concerning the business" (67). Furthermore, the managing member also has the right to "abandon" the production if s/he wishes. Upon abandonment, however, the managing member must liquidate all funds and accounts of the LLC (72).

As will be examined copiously in Chapter 4, the managing member(s) is (are) the surplus extracting capitalist. S/he has the complete authority and legal rights and responsibilities of the capitalist, s/he makes payments to secure his/her position as capitalist to writers, directors, theatre owners, conductors, the State, advertising, and so forth. Unlike other Marxian approaches that assert that the 'owners of the means of production' are the capitalists, NMCA gives the researcher an alternative. Ownership is not necessarily an essential element in determining who the capitalist is as is in the case in Broadway musical theatre. Indeed the 'managing member' qua the capitalist on Broadway does not necessarily 'own' the means of production, nor does s/he necessarily invest any of his/her own funds in the enterprise, nonetheless s/he is indeed the capitalist. This aspect of the analysis is counter to many traditional Marxists who believe the 'essential' criteria for determining whether a firm is capitalist or not focuses on ownership or power. To be clear, when using NMCA, the capitalist is the appropriator and distributor of surplus value, and ownership and power are not essential elements. Indeed, ownership and power are important issues and they may provide conditions of existence for capitalists, however the ultimate goal of NMCA is the eradication of exploitation, i.e., the appropriation of surplus value by someone other than its direct producer. As will be discussed, others Broadway agents wield power, while some own the means of production and the land, these simple facts do not make them capitalists, only agents in a capitalist structure.

2. The Landlords: Theatre Owners

All 33 Broadway theatres are concentrated in a small area of mid-town Manhattan—from the southernmost Nederlander Theatre on 41st Street to the northernmost Broadway Theatre at 53rd Street and Broadway, and from the Al Hirschfeld Theatre to the west near 8th Avenue and 45th Street to the Belasco Theatre which is east of 6th Avenue on 44th Street. Thirty-one of the theatres are owned and operated by three theatrical companies, the Shubert Organization with 17 theatres, the Nederlander Organization with 9 theatres, and Jujamcyn Theatres with 5 theatres. In 1997, Disney and Clear Channel opened the two remaining theatres, the New Amsterdam and the Ford Center, respectively. There are a total of 43,243 possible audience seats in the 33 theatres, averaging 1310 seats per theatre.[15]

The Producers, via license agreements,[16] rent one of the 33 Broadway theatres from the theatre owners for each production.[17] The rent payments for the theatre are generally negotiated at approximately 25–30% of the gross box office receipts (D. Farber, *Producing Theatre* 209–210).

Additionally, the theatre owners "traditionally keep the interest returns on advance sale of tickets" (Rosenberg and Harburg 33).[18] The Producer then pays most taxes, except real estate taxes ((D. Farber, *Producing Theatre* 486). The Producer also pays for all box office expenses, stage equipment, concessions, employee wages and payroll taxes, workers' compensation, and various insurance policies (491–495). The rental agreement may be for a specified period or indefinite. The theatre owner retains the right to terminate the agreement if box office receipts fall below a certain level for a certain period of time, usually two weeks; this is known as the "Stop Clause" (488).

Until the 1940s, most theatre owners were also the major Producers; however, by the end of World War II, some theatre owners decided to become only Producers, while others became landlords (Rosenberg and Harburg 32). During the 1970s, due to the economic recessions and increasing growth of the pornography industry in the Manhattan theatre district, theatre owners again began to produce shows so they might fill the 'dark' (empty) theatres. The trend has since reversed itself, and now it is common for theatre owners to also be the Producer, investor, or at least a significant stakeholder in a Broadway musical.

A. The Landlord's Employees

Until the 1960s, each Broadway theatre had its own 'house' orchestra, which played for every show in that theatre. Musicians were employees of the theatre owner in the traditional sense. The required size of the orchestra typically depended on the size of the theatre; theatres with more seats required larger orchestra than those with fewer seats. While this is not necessarily the case, there is a 0.9 correlation coefficient between the theatre size and the minimum musician requirement.[19] Attributable to the many modifications of the Broadway collective bargaining agreement and the requirement of non-traditional orchestras for many contemporary musicals, permanent house orchestras became obsolete; now musicians are hired on a per musical basis and the orchestra's composition is governed by the musical's genre and score. At present, the only vestiges from the musician/owner relationship are the minimum number of musicians required for a specific theatre and the ostensible theatre owner's title of employer of record.

Similar to other landlords, theatre owners are responsible for the maintenance and upkeep of their properties. In addition, the theatre owner provides and hires some of the staff necessary for legitimate[20] theatrical productions. They employ stagehands (carpenters, electricians, and curtain personnel), ticket sellers, theatre personnel (ushers, ticket takers, and doormen), maintenance personnel (custodians, porters, and elevator operators), clerks (mail clerks and telephone operators), heating and air-conditioning personnel, house [theatre] managers, house press agents, and musicians[21] (D. Farber, *Producing Theatre* 121–201). The theatre owners are technically the musicians' employers of record; however, this relationship is anachronistic for it is not a typical employer/employee relationship. Indeed, the musicians have little or no relationship whatsoever with the theatre owners, except that their paychecks are signed by the theatre owners. Broadway side-musicians[22] are hired/fired and supervised by a Music Coordinator (MC) who has a contractual agreement with the Producer for the provision of an orchestra for a specific musical. Although a member of the bargaining unit, only one musician, the conductor, is a direct employee of the Producer and has no direct relationship with the theatre owner. As an evolution of various collective bargaining agreements over the last 40 to 50 years, this convoluted arrangement is a remnant of a bygone era.

3. The Trade Association: The Broadway League

The Broadway trade association, the Broadway League[23] (the League) plays a distinctive role in the industry. Until recently,[24] every Broadway Producer, theatre owner, and general manager joined the League for an annual fee of $1000 for an affiliate membership and $1250 for an associate membership.[25] Like other trade associations, the League promotes and supports live Broadway by sponsoring marketing research, promotion of Broadway Theatre, educational events and the like. Furthermore it sponsors events meant to increase audience attendance at commercial theatrical events across the US as well as in Canada. While industry promotion is standard in most trade associations, it is only a secondary, possibly even a tertiary function of the League. What makes the League distinctive is that its primary function is to negotiate the thirteen Broadway labor union contracts and to represent the Producers and theatre owners as management in grievances and on joint labor/management committees. Such an institution is relatively unusual in that it is a collective of employers and eliminates the need for individual Production companies and theatre owners to negotiate, maintain, and enforce their own labor agreements.

By virtue of being a League member, every Producer and theatre owner agrees to the terms and conditions set forth in the 13 collective bargaining agreements. The internal structure and the requirements of the League are quite similar to that of a traditional trade union, but instead of representing the workers' interests, the League represents the employers' interests. The League's internal workforce also mirrors that of trade unions in that the League has an executive director, research staff, public relations personnel, attorneys, labor negotiators, and the other usual departments of enterprises and unions. Like trade unions, membership in the League is ostensibly voluntary; however, there is an implied pressure exerted by League members for all theatre owners and

Producers to become members by insinuating that League membership gives legitimacy from the theatre community to its members.

The very existence of the League contributes to the idiosyncratic nature of Broadway musicians' employment and may obscure the precise nature of the class structure in which they toil. The League's presence creates the illusion of mutual interests, both because of the cooperation a musical production requires[26] and because of the employment practices on Broadway. While the League is the institution that negotiates the collective bargaining agreements and acts as management for most other purposes, the League does not officially employ the Broadway musicians; rather, as mentioned above, the musicians are legally employees of the theatre owners. The fact that the theatre owners are designated employers does not mean that they are the surplus value appropriators. Neither the League nor the theatre owners appropriate surplus value. They both receive a payment from it in the form of dues and rent respectively, but these payments are to secure a condition of the Producers' existence as capitalist. The League is simply an agent of the Producer qua capitalist and the Theatre owners that promotes their interests.

4. The Workers: The Musicians

> Musicians are rarely thought of as workers. Instead, we tend to see them as entertainers and, more often than not, powerful celebrities rather than wage laborers. Or we tend to think of musicians as engaged in "play" rather than work. And yet, if we think about the work of making music and the context in which this work takes place, we cannot help but acknowledge the myriad ways musicians are affected by the whims and caprices of capital, the routinization of labor, and the often dehumanizing conditions of production. (Zinn, et al. 124)

In most capitalist workplaces there is a collective of workers who perform their various tasks to produce a good or service. This is true on Broadway as well. Many agents perform their individual responsibilities and tasks to ensure the production of the musical, from the actors and musicians to the ticket takers and theatre janitors. In the case of Broadway musicians, their specific task is to play the Production's music under the leadership and supervision of the conductor.

Of the 6200 full-time-equivalent[27] Broadway musicians, a maximum of 325 may hold a position in a Broadway orchestra at any given time.[28] Nevertheless, approximately 1100–1200 musicians are considered Broadway musicians because they work more than four weeks or thirty-two shows per year. The musicians' union, Local 802, made this designation to discern who is eligible to vote on various union issues regarding Broadway, such as the ratification of a collective bargaining agreement. There are basically two reasons why there are many more Broadway musicians than available positions. Firstly, most musicals do not last for an entire year and therefore theatres can house more than one musical per year. Thus musicians hired for the length of a theatre's musical production may not be hired for the next. For example, a musical opens at the Imperial theatre for three months for which 25 musicians are hired; after the show closes, another musical opens for nine months at the Imperial with 25 musicians. There is no requirement to hire any of the original 25 musicians; indeed it is more typical not to do so. Thus, even though there were only 25 positions for the year, 50 different musicians worked more than four weeks.

The second reason there are more musicians than positions is due to the considerable number of Broadway substitute musicians. A distinctive arrangement that Broadway musicians enjoy is the benefit of engaging fellow musicians to temporarily take their place in an orchestra. The full-time musician might wish to absent him/herself for a variety of reasons, including "obtaining occasional outside employment of limited duration; avoiding boredom which may occur in a long running show; and avoiding loss of identity in the marketplace (League, *Collective Bargaining Agreement* 16).[29] Each chair-holding Broadway musician is entitled to have a roster of five musicians who may substitute for him or her at any given time. The musician him/herself decides which musicians are to be included on his/her substitution roster. It is a very delicate process because today's chair-holder is tomorrow's substitute. Additionally, to avoid being disciplined, it is imperative that the chair-holding musicians only include substitutes who have similar talents and abilities. While a musician cannot hold concurrent Broadway positions, the same is not true for substitutes. Therefore, many substitutes are on multiple chair-holder substitution rosters that serve to further increase the number of performers that Local 802 considers Broadway musicians.

The demand for a Broadway positions far exceeds the number of jobs available, and therefore, the musicians through their union make persistent efforts and arguments to maintain or increase the number of Broadway positions. However, the musicians' attempts are restricted because of Producers' desire to minimize costs by reducing the labor force. One way the musicians secure the number of positions is by a stipulation in the Broadway Collective Bargaining Agreement that states the minimum orchestra size for each theatre. The size of a Broadway orchestra can range from a minimum requirement of three to nineteen musicians, including the conductor. The orchestra may include more than the minimum number of musicians, but more often than not, only the minimum are employed. Unfortunately for the musicians, the minimum requirement has decreased by 21.6% since the 1998 collective bargaining agreement. Theatre minimums are an extremely contentious issue on Broadway. Indeed, the principal issue in the recent strike (2003) by the Broadway musicians was over the minimum staffing issue. The Producers wanted to completely eliminate minimums, and the Broadway musicians wanted to retain them. The result of the strike was that now the minimums only range up to 19 in the largest theatres, down from 26.

Historically, the minimum required number of musicians was determined by the size of the theatre, with the larger theatres requiring larger orchestras. Now, however, that is not necessarily the case because of various negotiated compromises on the musicians' as well as the theatre owners' and Producers' parts. The theatre owners have an aversion to minimums because a large theatre may not be as attractive a rental as one with a lower staffing requirement. Meanwhile, Producers argue that it is they who should be making the staffing decisions because this decision is a creative one, which should be exclusively theirs to make.

As mentioned above, the most contentious issue during the 2003 negotiations and the subsequent strike was minimum staffing levels. The Producers and theatre owners accused the union of featherbedding and demanded total relinquishment of the minimums, a demand and accusation they had previously made during the 1993 and subsequent contract negotiations. The underlying issue is not actually staffing minimums, but rather management rights and workplace control by the Producers and their agents. Prior to 1993, if a production's orchestral body did not meet a theatre's minimum requirement, Producers hired musicians who did not actually play in the orchestra but were paid as if they did; these musicians were called 'walkers.' Using the media to their advantage during negotiations, the Producers effectively exploited these 'walkers' to make the union look like greedy featherbedders. Thus, the notion of 'walkers' is disadvantageous to the musicians' and their union's position in the press, which is generally quite attentive during Broadway negotiations.

Consequently, during the 1993 negotiations, the musicians agreed to a new clause in the collective bargaining agreement entitled "Special Situations" (League, *Collective Bargaining Agreement* 12).[30] This clause gave Producers the right to contest the minimum requirement if the show did not creatively need the minimum. Since the initiation of "Special Situations," there have been no 'walkers' on Broadway. Nonetheless, during subsequent negotiations in 1998 and 2003, the Producers and theatre owners insisted that the minimum requirement was an antiquated featherbedding union monopoly clause that needed to be eliminated. The union prevailed in 1998 but failed in 2003, and the minimums decreased considerably.[31] In return the League agreed to not open the issue of minimums until 2013.

Furthermore, the League spearheaded a vociferous assault during the strike with its allegation of the extreme expense of Broadway musicians. However, this claim is misleading and possibly a complete fabrication. For example, for the week ending January 5, 2003, the weekly orchestra costs including benefits were reported at $742, 316 while box office grosses were $15.2 million.[32] The average ticket price for the same week was $72.49 and the average portion of the ticket price paid to musicians was $3.70. Conversely, the "return of capital to Producers" is estimated at approximately 25% of a $100 ticket (Lennon, "The Issue").

A full time Broadway musician generally works eight performances per week with a maximum of three hours per show. Generally, the eight shows are spread over five or six days. If five days, then there are three days in which the musicians work two shows, a two o'clock matinee and an eight o'clock PM show. The same schedule is in place for the six-show week; only there are only two matinee days rather than three. Musicians receive 150% of their wages if they work more than eight shows per week or more than three hours per show (League, *Collective Bargaining Agreement* 14).[33]

As of March 1, 2004 the base or minimum scale wage for a musician playing one instrument is $1,355 per week plus 6.125% vacation pay and $50 for instrument maintenance or $1,488 per week. This does not include premiums or fringe benefits. Premiums for most responsibilities over those of a single instrument playing musicians include 30% for the associate conductor, 12.5% for playing an unrelated additional instrument,[34] $63.18 per week if the musician plays on stage, $42.13 per week if the musician wears a costume,[35] and 25% for playing an electronic instrument such as a synthesizer or an electronic drum machine.[36] Unlike other union workers, musicians are free to negotiate wages over the minimum scale wage with their employers. Most however, only receive the scale wages contractually agreed to, although some with special skills earn more than scale.

Broadway musicians are often highly educated, most are college graduates, many hold Masters' degrees and several hold doctorates, and therefore deserve and demand a wage commensurate with their talents and education. For example, Broadway musician and the current conductor of the Broadway show "The Lion King," Joseph Church, holds a Ph.D. in composing from New York University. Furthermore, with few exceptions, Broadway musicians are classically trained in prestigious programs such as Julliard. Indeed, the Broadway musicians receive salaries that are far more than most union workers earn, and as stated earlier, some musicians even earn more than the negotiated minimum scale wage.

A Broadway position is not necessarily a musician's first preference for employment; playing for philharmonics and opera companies is much preferred over Broadway. Nevertheless, Broadway positions have been and remain coveted jobs because these are full-time engagements with benefits and a certain level of job security. Broadway wages and benefits, particularly the pension plan, are extremely appealing in an industry in which jobs are unpredictable and insecure. The Broadway pension is particularly attractive in that the musicians receive a portion of the box office grosses. Over the last fifteen years, this portion has averaged over 20% of the musicians' salaries. For these reasons, thousands of musicians compete for a maximum of 300–400 positions on Broadway (Moriarity, "History").

Although a Broadway position is desirable, the working conditions are often substandard. Musicians work in orchestra pits that are typically dark, dirty, either too hot or too cold, and sometimes drafty. Frequently musicians are exposed to excessive sound levels, and they often inhale gases and fogs that are used for special effects. Additionally, similar to a factory assembly line worker, a Broadway musician is required to play the same notes at every performance, as a result carpal tunnel syndrome is becoming an ever-increasing concern of musicians.[37] These concerns will be further discussed in the next chapter.

5. The Foremen: The Conductors

> . . . in all labour where many individuals cooperate, the interconnection and unity of the process is necessarily represented in a governing will, and in functions that concern not the detailed work but rather the workplace and its activity as a whole, as with the conductor of an orchestra. This is productive labour that has to be performed in any combined mode of production. (Marx, *Capital Vol. III* 507)

Every Broadway musical is contractually obligated to engage both a conductor and an associate conductor; the collective bargaining agreement has provisions for payments to these musicians for the additional responsibilities that relate to these respective capacities.[38] The Producer directly hires the conductor; s/he is the only orchestra member who is not a direct employee of the theatre owner. The conductor and, in his/her absence, the associate conductor lead both the actors and the orchestra during a Broadway musical production. The actors and orchestra members take cues from the conductor so as to coordinate the smooth running of the production. Broadway conductors hold contradictory positions. On one hand, s/he has the role as conductor in which s/he assumes the function as the coordinator of music and acting. On the other hand, s/he is a supervisor who has the authority to reprimand and s/he is the final arbiter of a musician's substitution list, among other supervisory rights and duties.

In his/her capacity as the coordinator of music, s/he is a union member and is represented by the musician's collective bargaining agreement as such. Local 802 negotiates wages, benefits and working conditions on his/her behalf, like any other orchestra pit musician. In this capacity, the conductor acts much like a factory foreman, coordinating the acting and the music so it is pleasantly audible and viewable. As with any other musician, the conductor produces surplus value in this role.

At the same time, in his/her capacity as the supervisor, the League negotiates on behalf of the conductor. This role is not explicitly extensive;[39] however, conductors do wield slight power in this capacity in that s/he may reject a musician's choice of substitute (League, *Collective Bargaining Agreement* 16).[40] Moreover, to complicate things further, the conductor often assumes the role and responsibilities of Music Director (MD).

The MD is typically responsible for much of the transitional music, dance, voice and music arrangements, some orchestrations, and managerial tasks. In this capacity the conductor qua MD is considered management and the terms and conditions of his/her employment are NOT negotiated in the collective bargaining agreement, thus the MD position is not part of the bargaining unit. The Broadway MD represents a peculiar practice; typically union members in other industries who are covered by a collective bargaining agreement do not, or cannot, simultaneously hold management positions. Indeed, because of the conductor's (albeit limited) supervisory responsibilities and because of the dual role as MD, conductors could possibly be deemed legally excluded from the bargaining unit by the National Labor Relations Board.[41] But on Broadway things are not necessarily typical. As MD,[42] the conductor has significant creative control within the musical. S/he is often responsible for the entire musical score and trains the actor/singers. Moreover, the Producer hires the MD during the planning stage, well before the production comes to Broadway.

The fact that many conductors qua surplus producers simultaneously hold the MD position qua agents of the capitalist to ensure the maximum surplus is indeed an interesting phenomenon. One of NMCA's features is that it allows the researcher to understand the complexities involved with the various positions one holds. As will be discussed in greater detail in Chapter 4, the conductor qua MD holds two distinct class positions. Firstly, s/he holds the fundamental class position as surplus producer; while at the same time s/he holds the subsumed class position as a recipient of some of the surplus. Though these positions are contradictory, they are pedestrian on Broadway, and typically the persons holding the positions do not perceive the contradiction in that they prioritize their MD position and conducting is simply one of their responsibilities.

6. The Labor Broker: The Music Coordinator

> In show business it is less often true that the show is on and most often the case that the show is off. Being a union member does not guarantee jobs in a risky business. As any one knows who has ever worked the night shift or waited on tables, many of these dancers, actors, and musicians are 'between engagements.' (Rosenberg and Harburg 20)

As has been intimated above, the musicians' relationship(s) to the capitalist, the musical's Producer, is obscured by a variety of institutions that have emerged over time. One of the more significant obscurities is the role of the Music Coordinator (MC).[43] As mentioned above, the musicians are anachronistically employees of the theatre owners, but the theatre owner does not hire, supervise, or perform any of the usual managerial responsibilities associated with employers; music coordinators (MC) have this responsibility. The MC now hires all the Broadway orchestras, which seems to contradict the collective bargaining agreement, which clearly states that:

> The Employers shall engage all musicians required by them through [designated] Contractors, as heretofore. The [designated] Contractor for each show shall be selected by the Producer and Theatre Owner in consultation with Local 802. The Executive Board of Local 802 shall be immediately notified of each such selection and all such selections shall be subject to review by the Executive Board of Local 802 for the sole purpose of determining whether the Contractor has engaged in any conduct inimical to Local 802. The Contractor shall be a playing musician in the orchestra for the run of the show. (League, *Collective Bargaining Agreement 2*)[44]

Moreover, the MCs, in their capacity as MC,[45] are not employees of the theatre owners; the musical's Producers, i.e. the capitalists, engage the MCs. The MC's principal responsibility is to provide an orchestra for a Broadway musical that meets the specifications established by the Producer and his/her representatives. The MC must hire the minimum number of musicians required for each theatre as specified in the musicians' collective bargaining agreement.[46] He must also hire musicians who have the capability to perform in the specific genre of the musical that is specified by the Producer.[47]

Broadway MC's are a limited group of four to five men, thus they wield enormous power over the musicians as the 'gatekeeper' to jobs on Broadway. As of June 30, 2004 they include John Miller, Michael Keller, Seymour "Red" Press, John Monaco, and on occasion, Paul Gemigani. Misters Monaco and Press are approaching retirement and their workloads reveal this; as of June 14, 2004, each man had but one MC position.[48] Two Broadway music coordinators, John Miller and Michael Keller, are now quite prolific, with John Miller leading the way. As of May 2003, Mr. Miller is the MC of 50% of the Broadway musicals. Moreover, each MC is an active, dues-paying member of Local 802. Additionally, any of these men could at the same time be the MC and a playing musician in a show,[49] therefore giving the MC the dual position as surplus value producer and also a recipient[50] of the surplus value.[51]

As a rule, the only way a musician can be hired on Broadway is through an MC; therefore, if a musician does not have access to a coordinator, or if in the past the musician somehow antagonized him,[52] his/her chances of being hired on Broadway are negligible at best. Consequently, it is typically in a musician's best interest to maintain a tractable relationship with a music coordinator; this includes, among other things, avoiding grievances about contract violations and often complying with arbitrary, non-negotiated rules and traditions. The reason for this is primarily one of job security; musicians, once hired, are employed for the entire length of that particular show's run on Broadway unless the musician makes some egregious infraction of the collective bargaining agreement, violates work rules, or consistently performs less than satisfactorily. The employer however, must prove "just cause" and typically needs to produce evidence of progressive discipline[53] if s/he wishes to terminate a particular musician. Because MCs rarely, if ever have structured/detailed personnel files for each musician, termination of any Broadway musician during the course of a show is quite uncommon (Press, Interview).[54]

Most shows are extremely volatile and close after only a few performances. However, there are a few long-running exceptions like "The Lion King," "Phantom of the Opera," "Les Misérables," and "Cats." Nonetheless, historically, most musical shows ran for only a season, that is September through May (Moriarity, Interview). Still the longest running show, "The Phantom of the Opera," has been running for over 20 years, which is usually much less than a typical musician's work-life. So it is imperative to a Broadway musician's employment longevity to remain in the acquiescence of the MC. Essentially, if, during the course of a show, the MC finds a musician objectionable, the probability of being employed by that MC for another musical is slight at best. This is not only a perceived power position, it has been explicitly and openly acknowledged by the MCs themselves. In an interview with Mr. Press, he stated that he would not and has not reemployed musicians who "cause problems" in the orchestra pit. Press admitted that "problems" range from not taking suggestions from the MC about the hiring of substitutes to not getting along with fellow orchestra members to more serious infractions like sexual harassment (Press, Interview). When I asked Local 802 Past President Bill Moriarity about the extreme power the MC wields and what might the union do to change this relationship, he stated that this is the way it has always been done and neither he nor the union plan on changing that relationship. President Moriarity continued that he did not believe it was the union's responsibility to change how management operates or is organized (Moriarity, Interview). The Broadway musicians and their union are acutely aware of the relatively powerless position they hold vis-à-vis the MC when it comes to employment on Broadway. However, the musicians, the union and the MC himself accept the power wielded as standard practice and are currently making no efforts to change this arrangement. Therefore, the union through its own reluctance to change may indeed reinforce the Broadway musicians' positions as exploited workers.

The MCs perform the "subletting of labor" (Resnick and Wolff, *Knowledge* 153). Marx would deem them the "parasites between wage labor and capital" of Broadway musicals (153). Yet, although the MC is but an employee acting as an agent of the Producer, the MC's power vis-à-vis the musician is formidable and many of the problems and fears that the musicians confront daily can be attributed to the capriciousness of the MC. An elaboration of the problems the musicians encounter is found in Chapter 3. Furthermore, as will be revealed in the prototype in Chapter 4, within the NMCA framework the necessity of an MC all together will be superfluous.

7. The Union: Associated Musicians of Greater NY, Local 802 of the American Federation of Musicians

Why is the Broadway industry so highly unionized? For the same reason that several other industries are highly unionized: abusive exploitation by property owners and producers. (Rosenberg and Harburg 20)

As a condition of employment, every Broadway musician, including conductors, must become members of Local 802 by the thirtieth day subsequent to having first performed on Broadway (League, *Collective Bargaining Agreement* 1).[55] Local 802 currently represents every conductor, associate conductor, and side musician[56] on Broadway; in other words, there is a union density rate of 100%.[57] Like other U.S. unions, Local 802 is the musicians' sole representative and is responsible for negotiating the collective bargaining agreement, representing musicians in grievances, and occupying positions on the boards of directors of joint union/management health and pension funds.

Local 802 subscribes to the concept of business unionism, and for the provision of services, musicians pay annual dues as well as 3% of their wages in "work dues" to Local 802. Local 802 is a quintessential example of what Frank Annunziato considers "commodity unionism." He states, "contemporary American unions . . . have evolved into producers and distributors of a peculiar commodity which is called 'union representation'" ("Commodity" 9). Annunziato believes that when observing unions with a class perspective, the structure and operations of most if not all unions is itself capitalist. That is, unions hire wage laborers including professional staff and elected officials. The union subsequently sells these services to its customers qua members. In return for the commodity union representation, the customer qua members pay an exchange value in the form of dues. The executive board of the union is the first recipient of the dues and makes decisions on their distribution.

As an example of "commodity unionism" Local 802 employs wage labor as hired staff, and elected and appointed union officials. The Local 802 executive board makes all the decisions on surplus distribution, i.e., they vote on raises or promotions of staff, they negotiate collective bargaining agreements with the staff unions, they make decisions regarding capital improvements for the headquarters building on 48th Street and various other surplus value distribution decisions that the executive board believes will secure Local 802's conditions of existence. The surplus is created by the professional staff and sometimes by the union officers themselves through the collective bargaining procedure and its subsequent enforcement. Furthermore, Annunziato contends, that the union organizers are the marketers of union representation. Professional staff and the officers do most, if not all of the contract negotiations as well as the subsequent contract enforcement. Musicians rarely have any notable role in any of these processes. Indeed, each work area where the musicians are employed has a committee that is supposed to advise the professional staff and officers of their particular issues and needs,[58] however, in the final instance, the negotiations are not in the control of the musicians. During the 1998 Broadway negotiations for example, there was a significant presence of the theatre and Music Directors' (conductors) committees at most negotiation sessions. These committed volunteer members spent an exorbitant amount of time at the meetings and negotiations, although they were rarely, if ever called upon to testify or negotiate. These tasks were the sole responsibility of President Moriarity and Local 802 council, Lenny Lebowitz. The musicians and the conductors truly believed they had a significant input in negotiations; however, this was not the case. After a lengthy Friday afternoon bargaining session, President Moriarity and Council Lebowitz met with the League's attorney and struck a bargain—no union member or other professional staff was aware of this clandestine meeting which resulted in a new collective bargaining agreement. The committee members and professional staff only became aware of the deal the following day when summoned by President Moriarity to his office. The resulting deal excluded many of the so-called non-economic issues that the musicians and conductors thought important. President Moriarity, as with most other unionists, believes that wages, staffing minimums, and benefits are the most important issues for the members, therefore, if a deal is struck regarding those issues, all others become moot.

Annunziato also maintains that their members often view unions as "personal insurance" companies, not as sites for collective action (18). This is indeed the case with Local 802. Like most unions, many Local 802 members do not participate in union affairs and only come to the union in times of crisis, such as a grievance, contract negotiations, or a strike. Most of its members do not understand how the union operates or comprehend its role. Most of the Broadway musicians I spoke with during my tenure did not even understand the most basic union concepts—they viewed the union as some type of trade association, which they paid dues to for the pleasure of being allowed to work as a Broadway musician. There are very few resources allocated for educating the membership of Local 802 of the union and its role. This may be a conscious decision by the President and the executive board in order to retain their own positions as capitalists. This also strengthens the "ideological notion of the union and its staff as the sources of commodity production and distribution" (Annunziato, "Commodity" 18). That is, there is a consciousness by the musicians that they should simply be musicians and leave the labor issues to the professionals. This also reinforces Annunziato's claim that union members, in this instance the musicians, are consumers of a particular commodity namely union representation. Union members have no strong desire to change the status quo, even though the members might benefit from any changes in class structure.

Indeed, one obstacle to a class transformative agenda may be the Local 802 officials and Executive Board. Such an agenda may not be palatable to Local 802 officials because if Local 802's professional staff had a clear understanding of capitalist exploitation they could possibly challenge the capitalist class process within Local 802 itself. That is, if the Local 802 professional staff becomes aware of their own positions as exploited workers they may attempt to make changes in their own working conditions to the dismay of their employer.

Whatever the internal economic structure of Local 802, it has indeed made significant improvements for the Broadway musicians over the years. During the 1990s, for example, while other union workers' real wages were decreasing, the Broadway musicians actually experienced an increase in real wages. This increase of almost 13% from 1990 through 2002 can be seen in Figure 2.1 below. Additionally, the Broadway musicians realized substantial increases in fringe benefits, including pension contributions averaging 20% and improved health and welfare benefits. Nevertheless, the wage and benefit package notwithstanding, Broadway musicians experience many of the same problems and concerns as other union workers, such as staffing requirements, unsatisfactory safety and health standards, negligible job security, gender and race discrimination, sexual harassment,

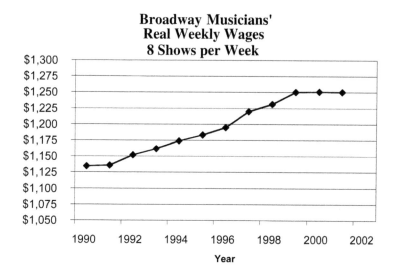

Figure 2.1 Broadway Musicians' Real Weekly Wages. 22 Jan. 2003 <http://www. bls.gov/cpi/home.htm>; (League, *Collective Bargaining Agreement*); and the author's own calculations using the Broadway musicians' collective bargaining agreements from 1990 and 1993.

and minimal participation in decisions affecting the work process. As will be discussed in the chapters that follow, there is a more expanded role the union can take that might counter these issues. However, this expanded role might be complicated by the fact that the internal structure of the union is capitalist. Within the NMCA framework, as will be seen, the union could take many of the responsibilities away from the MC and form orchestra collectives in which the union would therefore act as the workers' representatives in surplus distribution.

D. CONCLUSION

The Broadway musical is a composite of many different agents who use their experience, talent, and finances to present a product that has entertained millions for more than two centuries. The industry has a significant impact on New York City's economy, particularly in the tourism industry. Furthermore, many workers, directly or indirectly, depend on Broadway for their incomes and its economic impact is estimated at approximately $4.5 billion per year (League, *Broadway's Economic Contribution* 5).

Though there have been many musicals produced over the years, each has a similar basic structure, either the legal structure of a corporation or a LLC. The musical's Producer is the capitalist. The capitalist obtains a 'property' and subsequently rents a theatre from the theatre owner. Both the Producer and the theatre owner belong to the League, whose primary function is to negotiate collective bargaining agreements with the thirteen Broadway unions, including Local 802. The Producer hires the conductor and the Music Coordinator who sometimes collaborate to choose musicians for a Broadway musical. Nonetheless, it is the MC who hires the non-conductor (side) musicians, and typically, the conductor chooses his/her own associate conductor.[59] The musicians, each a member of Local 802, are employed for the entire run of the show. The Broadway musicians are capitalist surplus producers, the Broadway Producers are the capitalist surplus appropriators, and the League, the MC, and the theatre owners each receive a distribution of the surplus from the capitalist to secure some of the conditions of existence of the capitalist class structure.

Some perceive the industry as glamorous because of the notoriety and the stars, but many Broadway workers toil under harsh, sometimes hazardous conditions, as will be discussed in the following chapter. Like other capitalist workers, the musicians have little or no participatory role in their work environments, thus making their work, at times, barely tolerable. Furthermore, they cannot, or do not openly complain or file grievances regarding their working conditions because of the fear of negative reprisals, particularly from the MC, who tends not to hire or rehire dissident musicians. This fear is understandable given that there are essentially only two people who hire all the musicians on Broadway. Because of the fear of reprisal, it is often union representatives who file grievances on behalf of the musicians in order to maintain the complainant's anonymity. To date, a few musicians have taken some risks to improve their working condition by speaking out, however, most do not. Within the context of class transformation and the prototype that follows in Chapter 4, musicians' concerns might be better addressed and their voices heard without fear of reprisal of job insecurity.

Like other capitalist workers, many of the problems the Broadway musicians encounter can be linked to their fear of unemployment. The following chapter includes a discussion of the problems and issues the Broadway musicians confront on a daily basis. It also includes the response by the musicians and the union. Subsequently, in Chapter 4, there will be a complete NMCA of the various roles and class positions of the Broadway participants. A union-facilitated prototype for class transformation will then be offered. The primary objective of implementing the prototype is expunging exploitation; this occurs if the Broadway musicians appropriate the surplus value they produce. Furthermore, the argument will be made that, as a result of the union-facilitated class transformation, the fear of reprisal by the MC is extinguished. Many of the problems experienced by the musicians could be eradicated with class transformation, which would include eliminating any reason for a MC.

3   Subjects of Concern for Broadway Musicians

A. INTRODUCTION

Broadway musicians, like workers in other industries, confront workplace issues and problems on a daily basis. Workers' concerns are sometimes marginal, but more often than not, many concerns are quite serious, from the threat of unemployment to life-threatening injuries. As worker representatives, unions attempt to counter the negative aspects of the workplace through changes in the collective bargaining agreement, through the grievance procedure, or occasionally, through legal channels such as complaints to the Occupational Safety and Health Administration (OSHA) or the National Labor Relations Board (NLRB). Most of the time, unions react to problems that have already occurred or are imminent; unions tend not to have a precautionary or preventive approach and Local 802 is no exception. Local 802's basic strategy to counter the negative aspects of the Broadway musicians' jobs is not proactive; rather it is categorically reactive. Local 802 officials accept the status quo unless an imminent danger threatens a musician's health or job. Nevertheless, the amount of time that passes before any rectification is proposed and subsequently adopted is often protracted. To avoid these time-consuming reactive processes, Local 802 (as with other unions) could develop a strategic plan that seeks to address and ameliorate the problems and issues of the musicians before they are exacerbated.

The musicians, like any other workers in a capitalist structure, have serious concerns regarding their working conditions. As discussed in the previous chapters, the musicians' primary concerns are over safety and health, minimal worker participation in decision-making,[1] and job security. Like many other unions, Local 802 does not give the aforementioned concerns a significant place on their union agenda because, unlike wages and benefits, these issues are not considered 'economic' in the traditional union literature.[2] Although more attention was given to safety and health concerns in the 1998 and 2003 contract negotiations then ever before, they continue to be of secondary importance to Local 802 officials and the bargaining committee.[3] Moreover, the issues of worker participation and job security, while critical concerns of Broadway musicians, are completely absent from Local 802's proposals and its current agenda.[4]

This chapter is an investigation and examination of the various 'non-economic' concerns of the musicians including safety and health, worker participation, and job security. This is not to say that wages and benefits are of no consequence to the musicians. On the contrary, they remain salient. Nonetheless, Local 802's President, Bill Moriarity as well as other Local 802 bargaining team members gave little or no primacy to the 'non-economic' issues discussed in this chapter.[5] This chapter begins with a discussion of the safety and health concerns facing Broadway musicians including adverse health conditions caused by scenery and special effects, extreme sound levels, and repetitive work injuries. Secondly, there will be a discussion of worker participation or the lack thereof in the Broadway community. The final segment of this chapter will address the job security concerns Broadway musicians confront. Some of Broadway musicians' concerns remain hidden, even to the musicians themselves. The reactive strategies Local 802 employs have been mostly ineffective, thus necessitating an opportunity to suggest structural as well as class changes so that the musicians might improve their current as well as future working conditions. The primary objective of this chapter is to reveal concerns and issues that the Broadway Musicians face that are similar to those of workers in other industries, so that those workers too might benefit from this analysis.

B. SAFETY AND HEALTH

Unlike firefighters, police officers, and welders, a musician's job is not usually deemed a hazardous occupation. Indeed, there are few, if any, reports of serious bodily injury such as the loss of a limb, nor are there reports of workplace fatalities involving musicians. Nonetheless, one of the most critical concerns Broadway musicians confront is their safety and health. The three most pressing issues are: firstly, the inhalation of noxious particulates, gases, and vapors emitted from the special effects; secondly, excessive sound levels produced; and thirdly repetitive stress injuries.

The typical Broadway musician often works in a drafty, overcrowded, and confined orchestra pit,[6] while simultaneously forced to inhale possibly caustic particulates. To satisfy audiences' constant yearning for the spectacular, Producers have significantly increased their dependence on and use of special effects over the past 15 years, including the use of sophisticated pyrotechnic devices and obscure gases. Broadway Producers also believe that they are in direct competition with the motion picture industry, thus they now depend on the use of electronic instruments and sound devices that emulate the thunderous clamors of movie theaters. Furthermore, in the quest for uniformity and the increased length of many Broadway productions, Broadway Producers require the musicians to play exactly the same notes, in the same manner for every performance. Therefore, a relatively new concern of the musicians is repetitive stress disorders. The need to address these safety and health issues has become more acute over the last 15 years because of the ever-increasing dependence on the use of elaborate scenery and special effects, music amplification, and the increased longevity of Broadway musicals.

During the 1998 collective bargaining negotiations between Local 802 and the League, safety and health issues became a critical topic of discussion. Prior to 1998, the union and the employers did not address safety and health concerns for reasons that remain unclear; however, it is possible that they were not previously addressed because the problems were not as severe or, more likely, because complainants feared being labeled rabble-rousers.[7] In the 1998 collective bargaining agreement, "working conditions" provisions were limited to subjects like tuning pianos, toilet paper in the rest rooms, orchestra pit maintenance, and maintaining adequate orchestra pit temperatures (League, *Collective Bargaining Agreement* 11).[8] It is not implied here that these are somehow trivial issues; however, they are not as deleterious to a musician's health and career as the concerns discussed in this chapter.[9]

Until some of the safety and health issues became critical, the Broadway musicians, including some union officials, were unaware of their legal rights as to what types of care and information an employer is legally responsible to provide to workers. For example, when using certain substances in the workplace, employers are required to provide a "Material Safety Data Sheet" (MSDS) to employees for each substance to which employees are exposed. MSDSs are supposed to provide a list of the ingredients in any substance, caustic or otherwise, and their side effects. The sheets must be readily accessible to all workers who come in contact with the listed substances. However, this was not the case on Broadway, and after many requests by Local 802, when the union representative[10] was provided the MSDSs, many of the ingredients were not named because they are deemed 'trade secrets.' As a result of what the musicians believe to be an insufficient law, they insisted on prioritizing health and safety in their contract talks.

In the 1998 negotiations, Local 802 and the League agreed to a new, although not comprehensive "Health and Safety" clause in the collective bargaining agreement. This provision only addressed two of the most critical of the musicians concerns: the use of special effects and excessive noise levels. Experimental prototype safety devices were agreed to and, as a result, implemented. The new "Health and Safety" clause is as follows:

> In an effort to deal with the concerns of the parties about the use of certain smoke, fog, and/or pyrotechnics, as well as excessively high sound levels in the orchestra performance areas of the theatres, the parties have agreed to designate several productions as prototypes for the use of remedial ventilation or sound devices. The parties agree that consultants may be engaged for advice and that the cost of such consultants

or of any recommended ventilation or sound device to be used in the prototype production shall be paid for by either the Local 802 Health Benefits Plan or the Local 802 Sick Pay and Hospitalization Fund. The parties agree to recommend such expenditures to the Trustees of those Funds and such expenditures shall be subject to the approval of said Trustees. (League 2003, *Collective Bargaining Agreement*)[11]

This provision was a significant coup for the union and the musicians. It was the first of its kind in any of their collective bargaining agreements. More importantly, however, the provision made clear that health and safety problems persist in the Broadway orchestra pits and the League inevitably had to acknowledge their existence. This was a significant triumph over the past behavior; before the vociferous arguments made by the union and various musicians at the bargaining table, the League and most of its members tended to ignore or dismiss musicians' complaints as well as those of other theatre workers.[12] Prior to the 1998 collective bargaining agreement, the musicians implemented rudimentary procedures and unscientific jerry-rigged respiratory devices[13] in an effort to counter the inhalation of particulates and excessive sound levels. Unsurprisingly, musicians' home remedies proved to be ineffective, possibly even causing more damage to their health.[14] A complete discussion of the prototypes referenced above is forthcoming in the following two sections.

In the 2003 negotiations and the subsequent collective bargaining agreement, the musicians gained more comprehensive employer safety and health requirements such as union notification if special effects will be used in a show (League, "Memorandum 5").[15] The musicians gained contract language that far exceeds the law in that now the collective bargaining agreement requires "Right to Know" meetings and joint (Labor/Management) financial responsibility for consultants and safety devices. The seriousness of the health effects was the impetus for such an agreement. The following section includes a discussion of the specific problems musicians encounter to illustrate their gravity.

1. Scenery and Special Effects

Until the late 1980s, Broadway musicals were about the music, singing, and dancing, and they typically included one big 'production number' as the finale. Scenery and special effects tended not to be as elaborate as they are today; they were sophomoric attempts used to enhance the musical performance, not as the actual *pièce de résistance* as is now the case. Broadway Producers now believe that in order to compete with movies and other theatrical venues, musicals must be fantastic spectacles. The scenery has become much more sophisticated and much more prominent in recent years: from helicopters hovering over the stage as in "Miss Saigon" to a chandelier flying over the audience's heads as in "Phantom of the Opera."

Scenery does not usually have negative physical effects on the musicians' work environment; however, there have been infrequent incidences in which pieces of the scenery have fallen into the orchestra pit causing damage to instruments.[16] For a few productions, the Producers have installed netting over the orchestra pit to protect the musicians from falling objects. For musicians, the primary treacherous feat that they are called upon to do requires them to perform on stage, often on raised or moving platforms. Such occasional undertakings notwithstanding, ornate scenery has become the norm, amounting to an estimated 29% of the Producer's production budget, the same estimate for the total labor costs (League, *Broadway's Economic Contribution* 17). Nevertheless, while there are extra payments made to musicians for performing on stage, there is no provision in the musicians' collective bargaining agreement regarding any safety issues concerning scenery.[17]

Besides elaborate scenery, Broadway musicals have become increasingly dependent on the use of special effects such as glycol fogs, smokes, and pyrotechnics. In the past, musicals may have used some dry ice (solidified carbon dioxide) or special lighting to give a fog effect, but dry ice is now considered sophomoric, even amateurish.[18] Today's Producers opt for more sophisticated effects, and more musicals utilize special effects in one form or another. In a November 1997 survey of the Broadway musicians, 67% of the musicians reported that various types of smoke and fog special effects were used in their current shows.[19] Most of the problems with the use of these effects are due to their inhalation by the musicians. The problems are further exacerbated by the antiquated ventilation systems in most Broadway theatres, even the newer (refurbished) theatres do not have adequate ventilation systems that can purify the air of the toxins emitted by pyrotechnics, fogs, and gasses. The uses of special effects have had serious consequences on the health of the Broadway musicians, causing it to be a central topic during the 1998 and 2003 negotiations.

The most egregious perpetrator and abuser of special effects is Buena Vista Theatrical Ventures Inc., a subsidiary of Disney. Disney opened its first Broadway musical, "Beauty and the Beast," on April 18, 1994. This musical production used multiple pyrotechnic effects, along with various smoke and fog effects in the course of each show. "Almost from the day the show opened on Broadway in 1994, some of the performers said they began to get sick" (CNN Interactive). Within weeks of the opening Local 802 began receiving anonymous complaints from musicians about coughing, teary eyes, and unusual smells emanating from the stage into the orchestra pit. "By November 1995, several musicians were so concerned about their health that they asked for—and received—respirators from Disney's stage manager"(CNN Interactive). Local 802 officials, the show's Music Coordinator John Miller, and Disney began discussions about the various issues, and Disney agreed to make some minor changes in the special effects, and it also agreed to discontinue one of the worst offenders, the smoke from

Mrs. Potts' teapot. Nevertheless, the Disney compromises were insufficient and the musicians' complaints became more pronounced. "Beauty and the Beast" continued to use fireworks and smoke effects in the 91 year old Longacre theatre, which has an antiquated ventilation system and no protective devices such as an 'air curtain' (discussed below). Musicians continued to be concerned and continued to report respiratory illnesses; nonetheless, even with the degenerating conditions at "Beauty and the Beast," the show only recently closed.

The propylene glycol used in "Beauty and the Beast" is also used for "[o]rganic synthesis, antifreeze solutions, solvents, flavoring extracts, perfumes, coolant in refrigeration systems, hydraulic fluids, deicing fluids for airport runways, and cosmetics" (AOL®Hometown 1). Symptoms of exposure may include central nervous system depression and convulsions. In children, exposure can cause stupor, tachypnea, tachycardia, diaphoresis and seizures. This compound may be harmful through inhalation, ingestion or skin absorption. When heated to decomposition, it emits toxic fumes of carbon monoxide and carbon dioxide. To create the desired fog effects, the propylene glycol is heated to high temperatures to make it steam (fog) and then fans blow the fog across the stage. The fogs, however, do not remain on the stage; they are blown down into the orchestra pit as well as into the first rows of the audience.[20] Though the manufacturers' warning states that they do not recommend the use of this product in enclosed spaces or indoor arenas, Producers continue using it on stage regularly.[21]

Before information was provided to Local 802 and the musicians regarding the health risks posed by the contents of the special effects, the musicians believed they were being poisoned, as did many union officials. I observed the orchestra during 10 performances in the orchestra pit and twice in the first few rows of the audience to witness first-hand the conditions under which they toiled for eight performances per week. I also experienced some of the symptoms that plagued the musicians, such as coughing and teary eyes. By November 1996, 57% of the twenty-five musicians working for the Broadway production of "Beauty and the Beast" had been diagnosed with or complained of asthma, respiratory infections, shortness of breath, teary eyes, and other symptoms.[22] Furthermore, the oboist filed a successful workers' compensation claim for "occupational asthma."

To address this health hazard, one of the recommendations from the union officials was to mount a campaign to inform the public about the toxins emitted during the production. Initially most of the musicians flatly refused for two reasons, both relating to job security. Firstly, the musicians believed that any negative publicity would adversely affect audience attendance and, as a consequence, lead to the show's premature closing, which translates into unemployment for the affected musicians. The second reason, which was not explicitly articulated, was the fear of the musicians of negative repercussions by "Beauty and the Beast's" MC, John Miller.[23]

Mr. Miller notwithstanding, most "Beauty and the Beast" musicians appealed to Local 802 for support and advice on strategies to combat the negative side effects from the pyrotechnics and gases emitted during the production. Most, if not all, of the "Beauty and the Beast" orchestra members acknowledged a problem; however, some musicians remained steadfastly resistant to any union 'interference.' Nevertheless, Local 802 employed the services of investigators from the Irving J. Selikoff Center for Occupational and Environment Medicine at the Mount Sinai School of Medicine. Doctors and industrial hygienists evaluated the musicians on two separate occasions and the results were striking. Dr. Jacqueline Moline's November 18, 1996 report indicates that "[m]ore than half of the Musicians complained of chest tightness or wheezing. Nasal symptoms were noted in approximately 60% of the Musicians; eye irritation was noted in 75% of the Musicians" (Moline). The report was presented to Disney and adjustments were implemented, although Disney rejected the elimination of the use of any pyrotechnics and special effects during the performance.

Although the conditions persisted, many of the musicians remained wholeheartedly opposed to a public campaign to further their cause. In a February 1997 secret ballot poll of the orchestra nine of the twenty-five responses (36%) indicated that they very much opposed bringing the issue to the media's attention. However, in a November 1997 survey inquiring as to what issues the Broadway musicians wanted to prioritize in upcoming negotiations, health and safety concerns were overwhelmingly chosen.

During the 1998 Broadway musicians' negotiations, the League and Local 802 agreed that prototypes be developed to combat the uncomfortable and potentially harmful health effects caused by smoke and fog. An anti-particulate prototype device was developed by an industrial hygienist to address the problems. This device, an 'air curtain,' was installed in three theatres, the Imperial, the Palace, and the Majestic which were at the time housing the musicals "Les Misérables," "Beauty and the Beast," and "The Phantom of the Opera," respectively. Air curtains are made of polyvinyl chloride (PVC) piping that is lined with tiny perforations; when air is forced through the PVC, a curtain of air forms above the musicians' heads. Air curtains were placed on the rim of the stage, just above the orchestra pit and pumped air over the musicians and out towards the audience at stage level. The goal of the air curtain is to act as an invisible ceiling that prevents any particulates and/or gases from entering the orchestra pit.[24]

Keeping the gases and particulates outside of the orchestra pit is essential given a 2003 study, conducted by the University of British Columbia's School of Occupational and Environment Hygiene entitled "Atmospheric Effects in the Entertainment Industry: Constituents, Exposures, and Health Effects." The study's focus was on the safety of theatrical smokes and fogs when used by workers in the entertainment industry. Indeed, the researchers found that when theatrical workers are exposed to various smokes and fogs during the course of their work, they experience negative health effects. The study concluded when workplaces that use special effects are:

> [c]ompared to the control group, the entertainment industry employees had lower average lung function test results and they reported more chronic respiratory symptoms: nasal symptoms, cough, phlegm, wheezing, chest tightness, shortness of breath on exertion and current asthma symptoms, even after taking other factors into account such as age, smoking, and other lung diseases and allergic conditions. (Teschke, et al.)

The researchers recommend that glycol fogs, similar to those used at Broadway theatres, should be used sparingly. The researchers also stated that "[w]here theatrical smokes and fogs continue to be used, exposures should be monitored to ensure that control methods are working" (Teschke, et al. 3). Broadway musicians are not regularly monitored in any structured capacity; many musicians are monitored through their own private physicians, there is no collective endeavor for monitoring negative health effects by the musicians or Local 802.

Manufacturers of some of the effects maintain that their products should not be inhaled and warn against their use for purposes other than originally intended, that is not for use in enclosed poorly ventilated theatres. Even some of the 'safe' effects, such as mineral oil are safe if ingested, but not if inhaled. The UBC study cited recommends that "[t]he industry [theatre] should start working on exposure control plans for mineral oil in order to comply with regulations and to prevent the health effects observed" (Teschke, et al.). Furthermore, as addressed above, the Material Safety Data Sheets continue to exclude various ingredients that are deemed 'trade secrets' and the manufacturers of these products adamantly refuse to provide this information to their employees. Finally, the long-term health effects remain unknown. "Right to Know" meetings are a beginning, but they typically provide insufficient information to the workers as to what substances they are working with and the side effects of exposure.

Whether or not the air curtains stopped the miasma from the effects from entering the orchestra pit continues to be debated. According to the musicians, the air curtain prototype installed in the Palace theatre to combat the smoke and fog was ineffective (Lennon). Because the musicians continue to experience negative health effects due to smoke and fog, the Broadway musicians proposed an outright ban on the use of smoke, fog, and pyrotechnics during any production. Although the proposal was not accepted outright, new, more protective contract language was developed and is now being implemented. According to some musicians, air curtains made no noticeable change to the amount of particulates entering the orchestra pits, while others said there was only a moderate improvement. Moreover, the sound engineers insisted that the air curtains be must turned off at various times during the show because they made an almost inaudible humming noise—thus defeating the purpose for their installation. Thus, no 'air curtains' have been installed in subsequent musical productions. Nevertheless, the 2003 collective bargaining agreement does not necessarily reflect the reality of the situation. The new 2003 Memorandum of Agreement states that:

> The following prototype studies involving sound levels and smoke and fog abatement proved to be successful: *High Society* at the St. James for sound control, *Les Misérables* at the Imperial for glycol smoke/fog effects *The Phantom of the Opera* at the Majestic for dry ice smoke/fog effects. (League, Memorandum 2003)[25]

There was no agreement as to the successfulness of the air curtain at the Palace Theatre when "Beauty and the Beast" was housed there, and no air curtain has been installed in the Longacre Theatre, the subsequent home of "Beauty and the Beast."

Broadway musical productions continue to incorporate elaborate scenery and special effects, often with what seems to be little or no concern of the workers' health and the possible consequences of implementation of the effects, despite the best efforts of Local 802 and the musicians. While many shows choose not to use such flamboyant effects, anecdotal evidence from the Producers implies that their use is positively correlated with a show's longevity.[26] Claiming that sensational and extravagant movies and television shows are their main competition, Producers argue that the effects are necessary to remain competitive in the theatrical industry to meet audience expectations. Furthermore, as discussed in the next section, the Producers also maintain that technologically enhanced music is necessary to remain competitive with other theatrical venues, again with little if any concern for workers' health.

2. Sound Levels

Over the past two decades, Broadway musicians have been increasingly concerned with the extreme sound levels they tolerate while working. The increased volumes are due to a variety of sources such as amplification, electronic instruments, orchestra pit configuration, the size of the pits, and enclosure[27] of the pits (Babin). Although the Occupational Safety and Health Administration (OSHA) has set limits regarding acceptable sound levels, these standards were designed to address issues in factories and manufacturing plants and, therefore, do not address the unique concerns of musicians. On the other hand, the American Conference of Governmental Industrial Hygienists (ACGIH) considered musicians' distinctive circumstances. The ACGIH recommends lower exposure levels than OSHA, and researchers and industrial hygienists believe that "[g]enerally, musicians should verify that sound levels do not exceed 90 dBA[28] for any period of time" (Audible Difference). Table 3.1 compares OSHA and ACGIH acceptable protracted sound level exposures.

Table 3.1 Permissible Noise Exposures

Duration per day, hours*	OSHA Sound level dBA slow response*	ACGIH**
8	90	85
6	92	88.75
4	95	90
3	97	92.5
2	100	95
1	105	100
1/	110	105
1/4 or less	115	115

Sources: US OSHA. "Occupational Noise Exposure. 1910.95." 20 June 2000 <http://www.osha.gov/pls/oshaweb/owadisp.show_document?p_table=STANDARDS&p_id=9735>   and Local 802 internal reports from Angela Babin, M.S. Industrial Hygienist.

Since 1992, Local 802 has employed the services of Angela Babin, an Industrial Hygienist who has tested various Broadway musical productions for excessive sound levels. Table 3.2 below illustrates a sample of shows she tested for excessive sound levels in the 1990s.

Table 3.2 Broadway Sound Levels

Show	Average (dBA)	Maximum (dBA)	Performance Length
Joseph	101.00	115.5	2:05
Damn Yankees	94.88	114.0	2:41
Big (1st visit)	94.04	115.6	2:28
Beauty and the Beast	93.18	111.7	2:30
How to Succeed in Business	91.81	110.2	2:42
Big (2nd visit)	90.89	109.1	2:29
Sunset Boulevard	89.35	113.2	2:31
Miss Saigon (2nd visit)	88.35	104.5	2:38
Phantom of the Opera	87.57	107.5	2:28
Miss Saigon (1st visit)	84.08	107.5	2:20
Tommy	83.88	107.2	2:26

Source: Babin, Angela, *Art Hazard News*, 19. 4, (1996):1.

The average length of the Broadway musicals tested is approximately two and one-half hours. Musicians play eight shows per six or five-day week; this means that Broadway musicians play two shows per day twice or three times weekly. As table 3.2 indicates, each show tested exceeded the maximum suggested guideline of 90 dBA for musicians; however, only one show "Joseph" exceeded the OSHA standard for 2.5 hours. Moreover, on matinee days (two shows in a day), four shows exceed the six-hour threshold. Of course, if we apply the stringent ACGIH levels, 11 more shows can be added to the excessive noise perpetrators. Additionally, a typical Broadway musician performs or practices during the time that s/he is not performing on Broadway, thus his/her noise level threshold is further reduced.

Ms. Babin also performed audiometric testing on the fifteen "Joseph" musicians. She reported that "9 of the 15 musicians exhibited some hearing loss in the 4000, 6000 or 8000 hertz range, an indication of noise induced hearing loss. Five of those 9 players exhibited bilateral hearing loss" (Babin 1). Moreover, according to a New Zealand Study of over 200,000 people:

> Exposure to sounds at 100–110 dBA can cause damage after approximately 15 minutes. At 110–120 dBA damage can occur with exposures of less than 30 seconds duration. Many musicians are at risk of hearing loss because their ears can be exposed to average levels of 90 dBA and peak levels of 110–120 dBA during a musical performance. (University of Aukland)

Hearing loss can be detrimental to a musician's career; for example, even the slightest losses can affect a musician's ability to tune his/her instrument. This would not only cause embarrassment for the musician, it could also mean the end of his/her life's vocation.

Sound level restrictions were significant issues in Local 802's 1998 health and safety contract proposals to the League. The League and Local 802 agreed to a sound control "prototype" device to be implemented in the Saint James theatre for the production of "High Society."[29] Moreover, although not contractually obligated, a similar sound control device was installed at the Broadway Theatre for the production of "Miss Saigon." The sound devices seemed more successful in their objective than the air curtains. Basically the sound control 'device' was simply specially designed padding that was installed in strategic points in the orchestra pit to absorb excess noise.[30] According to Local 802's monthly newspaper, the *Allegro*, both sound devices were successful. The article states that:

> ... the sound treatments at both "High Society" and "Miss Saigon" were judged a success in significantly reducing sound levels and improving the overall sound of the orchestra. It was noted, however, that addressing such problems quickly is crucial, since years of exposure to unsafe sound levels prior to the installation at "Miss Saigon"

compounded the difficulty in resolving the problems and ultimately compromised the degree of the sound treatment's success. (Lennon, "Evaluate Health and Safety")

However, no subsequent devices of this type have been installed in other theatres. Health concern from exposure to excessive sound levels, as mention above, is further exacerbated by the length of time a musician or any worker is required to be in the situation. As previously noted, many Broadway musicals are running longer than their historical counterparts; thus hearing injuries are more likely to become more pronounced. Furthermore, shows' longevity also can contribute to other health problems like the repetitive stress disorders which will be discussed in the next section.

3. Repetitive Stress Disorders

As of August 1998, Broadway musicians reported no specific repetitive stress disorders cases to the union. Nonetheless, experts contend that musicians are subject to these disorders. Musicians' playing techniques are often not natural movements and, therefore, place undue strain on various parts of their bodies, particularly their fingers and hands. Broadway musicians repeat the same notes during each performance, sometimes for many years. Historically, Broadway musicals survived for only a 'season;'[31] however, this is no longer the case; some shows have been open for multiple seasons, even years. Although now closed, "Cats" ran for almost 18 years, "Les Misérables" for 16 years, and "A Chorus Line" for 15 years, moreover, "Phantom of the Opera," a 20-year-old show that continues to perform to sell-out crowds. With the increase in show longevity, there is associated risk of repetitive stress disorders, such as carpal tunnel syndrome (CTS).[32]

Musicians in general, but particularly theatre musicians, are exceptionally susceptible to repetitive stress disorders. Violinists and cellists report pain that is due to particular stress on their fingers and awkward, repetitive bow movements (Peiken). Pianists and drummers are equally susceptible, and players of other instruments are not immune (Fusco). As reported in *Allegro*:

> Any job that requires vigorous use of the hands in the same way for prolonged periods of time can cause CTS. Among those at risk are mail sorters, gardeners, supermarket checkout clerks, hairdressers, autoworkers and musicians—and, among musicians, especially pianists, violinists, bassists and drummers. Computers are a prime cause of repetitive strain injuries and their use can increase the risk for musicians, many of whom [sic] compose and handle their business affairs on the computer. (Fusco)

Although many Broadway musicians may not recognize that the pain they are experiencing might be due to their occupation, it is believed that this problem will escalate in the near future, thus making it an issue that must be addressed by the union in future negotiations. Local 802 did not address repetitive stress disorders during the 2003 negotiations with the League, which might be considered naïve given a musician's propensity to these types of disorders (Culf).

Like many of the topics that affect Broadway musicians, repetitive stress disorders hitherto have been ignored; concerns like this will customarily be addressed only when a crisis emerges, and such a crisis might lead to an increase in the amount of reported injuries or an increase in 'Workers' Compensation' cases. While Local 802 officials continue to confront other musicians' health and safety issues with some success, the remedies are often reactive, essentially a response to musicians' complaints. To adequately protect the best interests of the musicians, Local 802 might be more proactive. The union could begin by taking positive steps to educate the musicians about their susceptibility to repetitive stress disorder and other injuries, or they could negotiate terms in the collective bargaining agreement to counter present or future problems.

Local 802's reactive response to workers' concerns is relatively typical of most unions operating in a capitalist class structure; the employer (exploiter) dictates the conditions and the workers respond. At least in a union situation, the response might be structured and addressed through the collective bargaining process; in a non-union environment this is usually not the case. Therefore, with a union in place, there is a special opportunity for structural change within the context of the collective bargaining agreement. If the union adopts a class transformative strategy/agenda, then these concerns might be addressed in a more expeditious and fruitful manner. Conversely, if the union rejects a class transformative agenda, it is by default reinforcing a condition of existence for the capitalist class structure. Not making public or grieving health and safety issues has secured the capitalist's position as capitalist by reinforcing the notion that workers are obligated to the capitalist to produce surplus value without concern for their health and safety. Additionally, as the capitalist Producers' contend, their profits would be compromised if they were forced to refrain from using special effects and technologically enhanced sound effects due to the competition from other venues in the entertainment industry such as motion pictures.

Capitalist workers, like the Broadway musicians, are often subject to the capricious decisions made by their employers. These decisions, as we have seen in the discussion above, can have serious health effects on the workers. Moreover, capitalist workers are not afforded the opportunity to be part of the decision making process; their only role in the process is to obey the decisions or experience the consequences, that is termination of employment. If workers, including the Broadway musicians, were to be included in the decision making process regarding their working conditions, they might not be subject to such harsh conditions. Nevertheless, it is not the nature of a capitalist to initiate worker participation, thus it is imperative for the workers to insist on their own levels of participation. Broadway musicians only tangentially participate in capitalist decisions through their collective bargaining agreement, which puts some constraints on the Producers qua capitalists. However, as will be argued below, worker participation on Broadway is indiscernible.

C. WORKER PARTICIPATION

1. Voice

Broadway musicians sometime have the erroneous impression that they have a "voice" in the creative process and their work environments (Hirschman). The musicians may give suggestions, but they certainly have no authority for the implementation of any proposals or any guarantee that their ideas will be even heard by the Producers. Simply stated, the Broadway musicians are similar to workers in any capitalist structure; they are given set tasks, they are told how to perform said tasks, and they are expected to complete them in the manner and time allotted by management. Specifically, the MC hires the musicians, they are handed the musical score, they may have three or four rehearsals prior to the first preview, and then they perform what is dictated to them by their superiors. One exception to this is the conductor; the conductor has limited participatory role in the creative process and work environment as stipulated in the collective bargaining agreement. Moreover, the conductor often assumes the managerial role as Music Director or Musical Supervisor, and in this capacity, s/he has a true voice and authority with regard to the musical production. As of June 20, 2004, of the 20 open musicals, 17 of the conductors simultaneously held the position of Music Director. Nonetheless, the majority of the musicians do not have a respected voice. Therefore, these musicians will be the focus of this section.

Lack of participation in the work process is not uncommon in a capitalist class structure. Capitalists give their workers set tasks, the workers perform those tasks or risk unemployment; in return for their efforts workers receive wages for their labor and then go home only to return and repeat the same process the next workday. Within most capitalist enterprises, worker participation is negligible at best.[33] This situation has become the accepted standard mode of production in many, if not most, US workplaces as well as in other nations.[34] There are few who challenge capitalism; most people simply accept capitalism is the most efficient class process and that it is necessary if workers want to remain working. Moreover, in the name of 'economic development,' government officials on every level encourage and support encroachments of capital. Alternative class processes are not suggested or they are summarily rejected as some sort of radical anti-American agenda. Moreover, and possibly worse than the mere acceptance of capitalism by the general public, the US labor movement has accepted the capitalist status quo and has also rejected most radical agendas. Unions typically do not challenge the authority of management control; indeed there are "management rights" clauses in most collective bargaining agreements, which consequently reinforce capitalism in US workplaces.

Like most other unions, Local 802 makes no challenge to the capitalist class structure; consequently the union inadvertently reinforces Broadway capitalism. Local 802 does not consider itself as anything more than a service union, and their acceptance of the status quo reinforces the position of the Producer qua capitalist and the workers (musicians) exploited positions. Moreover, when asked about the possibility of class transformation on Broadway, former Local 802 President Bill Moriarity summarily dismissed the conversation, and stated that the union is only in business to protect the workers, not change the way Producers do business (Moriarity, Interview). For example, while preparing their proposals for the 1998 negotiations, the Theatre Committee, which includes representatives from most Broadway musicals as well as 'at large' members, suggested that the musicians would be better served if they had more decision-making power in the creative process. Additionally, the committee also put forward a scheme to mount quasi-productions for the purpose of educating young (potential) audiences about musical theatre. Both suggestions were discussed at length in committee; however, when presented to President Moriarity and his assistant Bill Dennison, they outright dismissed both proposals. They curtly claimed that what the committee proposed were functions of management and not in the union's purview. Both proposals were never given to the League.

Although Local 802 perceives itself as liberal and progressive, it is in reality a pragmatic service union, not a revolutionary institution.[35] Furthermore, the union accepts without question the capitalist's role and often explicitly repudiates any dissenting arguments from its members. Union officials have made it clear to the members that they will not challenge management rights within the collective bargaining agreement. Consequently, the union officials themselves furthermore diminish the possibility of class structural change. For example, the union does not challenge the fact that Broadway musicians are explicitly prohibited from producing a musical. This limits Local 802's choices in how to respond to capitalist exploitation, in that it prevents musicians from taking the role as surplus appropriators and its subsequent distributors. This issue is specifically addressed in the Collective Bargaining Agreement between the League and Local 802:

No musicians shall be engaged who are the theatre owner, producer, general manager, relative or employee of the theatre owner, producer, contractor or any Local 802 official, the spouse of the general manager, producer, theatre owner or the contractor or any Local 802 official. (League, *Collective Bargaining Agreement* 3)[36]

Local 802 ostensibly implemented this clause to avoid potential conflicts of interest.[37] There has never been a challenge to this clause, and even if such a challenge were brought forward, it too would be categorized as a non-economic issue because it does not directly involve wages or fringe benefits. Typically, issues that are deemed non-economic are not given a high priority during negotiations. Moreover, because of its class-blindness, the union does not reorganize or discuss economic issues of surplus appropriation and distribution thus perpetuating Broadway musicians' exploitation. This clause is but one example of a roadblock to class structural change imposed by the union itself. In effect, the clause prohibits the workers from being capitalists themselves or surplus appropriators in some other class arrangement.[38]

2. Minimum Requirements Redux

The illusion of 'voice' is further exacerbated by the musicians' unwitting notion that maintaining a minimum musician requirement in the orchestra pit gives them voice in the creative process. As discussed in the previous chapter, a long-standing stipulation in the Broadway musicians' collective bargaining agreement is a minimum requirement of musicians in each Broadway theatre. This issue is and historically has been one of great contention. The union and its members maintain that in order to ensure the quality of live music in Broadway theatres, a particular number of musicians must be hired for each show.[39] Indeed, the March 2003 strike was primarily about minimums. The musicians accused the Producers of killing 'live music' on Broadway. In fact the union members orchestrated a mock New Orleans style funeral Broadway in the middle of Times Square to illustrate live music's death (the corpse was 'live music'). The Producers asserted that they should have complete creative control over the musical, and therefore, they should determine the appropriate orchestra size. However, to assert their creative voice, the musicians attempted to preserve the minimum requirement.

Meanwhile, the Broadway musicians consistently maintain that the minimum requirement is not an issue of job security; rather the musicians argue that minimums are necessary to preserve the integrity of the musical. As previously mentioned Broadway musicians as a group are very talented, educated, and well trained, many classically. Most are resolute that each performance is their best; the quality of each performance is of utmost importance to the musicians. They argue that the fewer musicians in a pit, the poorer the quality of the music. According to Local 802 President, Bill Moriarity:

> The competing claims that both the League and the union made regarding the creative process and how decisions are made within that process should be more closely examined. The choices made on size and use of orchestras directly affect the composers, orchestrators, performers and musicians and underpin the artistic credibility of a musical production. (Moriarity, Interview)

The musicians fought stalwartly to convince the press and the public that minimums are vital to the integrity of the musical, and they had some success, particularly with the other Broadway unions that honored the musicians' picket line. The Broadway musicians tried convincing themselves that the minimum requirement somehow gives them creative control; however, this is subterfuge. The only thing the minimum requirement gives them is a minimum number of musicians in the pit, nothing more. The Producers maintain creative control, and the latest collective bargaining agreement language ensures that.[40]

D. JOB SECURITY

Like workers in other industries, Broadway musicians confront various threats to their job security. The threats take different forms, such as, the reduction of the number of musicians hired for each production, the replacement of musicians with machines, and the implementation of dubious managerial practices. Broadway musicians have union protection, a 100% unionization rate, and musicians cannot be terminated after the second rehearsal except for 'just cause.'[41] They are employed for the entire length of the specific production for which they are hired. That is, if a musician finishes the second orchestra rehearsal and is not terminated, s/he has the position for the entire life of the show, whether it survives for two months or fifteen years. Yet their jobs remain tenuous. Local 802 has made every effort to ensure musicians' job security; however, the Producers constantly challenge the union's efforts because they are determined to minimize costs and want total control of the production. This approach is comparable to any other private capitalist industry. This section includes discussions of the three most egregious affronts to the job security of Broadway musicians: the decrease in the minimums, the use of electronic devices, and the hiring/rehiring practices of the MC.

1. Minimums and Job Security

As discussed previously, all musical productions must include a specified number of musicians, now ranging from three to nineteen per musical, which represents a 32% decrease in the minimum requirement since 1990. It would be imprudent to not include a brief discussion of minimums when examining Broadway musicians' job security or the lack thereof. While the musicians and their union officials emotionally testify that the minimum requirement must remain in the collective bargaining agreement because of the threat to live music and the musical integrity of the production, there remains the tacit reality that minimums secure the number of working musicians on Broadway.[42] The musicians' challenge is to persuade the public and others to believe that retaining the minimum requirement is critical for quality Broadway musicals. Conversely, it remains a fact that the minimum requirement directly affects the number of available positions for Broadway musicians. The Producers contend that they hire the necessary number of musicians for a creatively sound quality musical while they actually only hire the minimum required by the collective bargaining agreement. For example, in February 1998, of the 13 open Broadway musicals, only one orchestra, "Phantom of the Opera," employed more musicians than the minimum required.[43] The Producers adamantly contend that minimums are not about creative control, only staff size. While the musicians were successful in their 2003 public campaign for 'live music,' they still failed to retain previous staffing levels. Now if all of the 32 theatres were occupied by musical shows, 392 musicians would be required, which represents a 22% decrease from the 1998 minimum of 500.[44] Consequently, while the musicians continue their quest to retain minimums because, as they maintain, minimums are vital to the musical's integrity, the Producers' resist. On the other hand, most theatre enthusiasts agree that the Producers would not be able to maintain the sound of a full orchestra without the minimum requirement or the utilization of electronic instruments to supplement or replace the orchestra.

2. Electronic Instruments

It is remarkable that the demand for live musicians on Broadway remains, given the available alternatives. However, the demand for live Broadway musicians has substantially decreased since the introduction of labor saving devices such as electronic synthesizers, drum machines, and more recently, 'virtual orchestras' (VOs).[45] These technological advances have the capability of reproducing music that sounds like an entire orchestra, a section, or at the very least, enhancement of a particular section.[46] For example, keyboard synthesizers are readily used in most musicals. These instruments not only replace pianos and organs, but they also have the capability to reproduce the sounds made by the string, the horn, or the woodwinds sections among others. This gives rise to a decreased demand for musicians who are substituted with electronically enhanced sections. The Producers contend that synthesizers complement orchestras, while the musicians contend they erode jobs. Local 802 and the League negotiated a compromise in the collective bargaining agreement that states that in a legitimate Broadway musical, a premium of 25% must be paid to the player of any electronic instruments. The 25% premium was intended to penalize Producers and create a disincentive for the use of electronic devices that replace working musicians. However, over the years, electronic devices in the orchestra pits have become increasingly more common; synthesizers are used in most, if not all Broadway productions.

The debate between musicians and employers over the use of electronic music is long-standing. In the late 1920s and early 1930s electronic music was introduced in movie theaters. Movie theaters that once employed many (thousands) musicians around the country terminated and replaced them with recorded music. This, the employers argued, prevented any human error and provided a better product. Even in the 1930s, Local 802 and then AFM president Joseph Weber developed a public relations campaign that degraded electronic or '*canned*' music. Weber argued, "'art can not be mechanized' and that recorded music 'can not approach the genuine article'" (Zinn, et al. 134). By 1936 the campaign failed, musicians were routinely fired and recorded music in the movie theaters became the norm. The musicians tried to resist by instituting a strike in the summer of 1936 through July 1937; however, the musicians failed and the Local 802 executive board called the strike off.

Interestingly, the Broadway musicians initiated a similar campaign in the latter part of 2002. Faced with an expiring collective bargaining agreement and realizing that the League would strenuously argue against the minimums clause in the contract, Local 802 developed and implemented its "Save Live Broadway" Campaign. On March 6, 2003, the campaign escalated to a strike by the musicians. The musicians instituted a website (www.savelivebroadway.com), a media blitz, and a petition signed by over 30,000 people including luminaries such as Patty Duke, Sally Struthers, Bette Midler, Tony Danza, Christine Ebersole, Joel Grey, Chita Rivera, Bebe Neuwirth, and Robert Goulet. Furthermore, through the conventional picketing of the Broadway theatres and an unconventional staged Dixieland mock funeral in Times Square, the musicians were able to convince the public that the Producers were threatening 'live music.' The Producers were prepared for the musicians to strike, in fact, they spent hundreds of thousands of dollars to rehearse and implement a new technological device known as the 'virtual orchestra' (VO). On March 6, 2003, the musicians struck and the VOs were installed and ready to replace the musicians if the need arose. The musicians were reluctant to strike because as so many audience members are tourists who probably are not accustomed to live music, the Producers' use of the canned VO music might go unnoticed. Unlike the 1936–7 strike, the 2003 stoppage successfully avoided VOs, but not necessarily because of the public support for live music on Broadway. Rather, the musicians were able to shut down Broadway and remove the threat of being replaced with the robotic VOs only due to the unexpected honoring of the musicians' picket lines by the members of such unions as Actors' Equity and the International Alliance of Theatrical Stage Employees (Moriarity, Interview). The four-day strike was costly to both the workers and the Producers; workers lost wages and benefits payments, and according to the League's executive director Jed Bernstein, the strike cost the Producers $1.2 million per performance, and $7 million per performance for the ancillary businesses, such as taxies, restaurants and hotels (Pogrebin). The strike, which 'darkened' 18 musicals, was so significant to New York City's economy, that the City's mayor, Michael Bloomberg compelled Local 802 and the League to meet at Gracie Mansion[47] with a mediator appointed by the Mayor. Mayor Bloomberg instructed both sides not to leave the bargaining table until an agreement was reached. Local 802 and the League did just that and ended the strike after negotiating through the night (Pogrebin). In the end, there was no obvious winner of the strike. Moreover, the successfulness of the "Save Live Broadway" campaign remains ambiguous because the outcome of the strike was greatly influenced by the fact that the actors, stagehands, and other Broadway unions honored Local 802's picket lines. If the other Broadway unions crossed the musicians' picket line, the outcome would probably have been quite different, because Broadway musicals would have proceeded as usual, only with "virtual" orchestras, that is shows would have remained open using taped music instead of live musicians. This use of recorded music could have set the precedent that the musicians are relatively less important than other theatre workers.[48] However, due to the solidarity between the unions, the musicians' relative importance to the musical became a non-issue.

Indeed, the threat of using VOs was utterly viable and if the actors and stagehands had crossed the musicians' picket line, the VOs would have been used and thus, the strike would have been a complete failure. The Producers had them in place before the strike because they knew that the 2003 negotiations would be quite contentious given their absolute insistence on the eradication of the minimums clause. Both Local 802 and the League were obstinate concerning the minimums' clause with the union wanting no change and the League vying for its total elimination. The 2003 negotiated clause now includes the statement that "[t]he parties recognize that live music is essential to the Broadway musical experience" (Memorandum 2003). This article is the contractual embodiment of that commitment,[49] therefore retaining live musicians in Broadway theatre at least until 2010 and giving the Broadway musicians some aspect of job security. The use of 'electronic' musicians, however, is not the only threat to musicians' job security, the MC as agent for the capitalist Producers also poses challenges for the Broadway musicians.

3. Music Coordinators

A cursory reading of the collective bargaining agreement would give one the impression that the musicians enjoy many safeguards against being arbitrarily terminated by their employers, and indeed they do, at least for the production in which they are currently employed. However, all Broadway musicians' job 'security' dissipates once a production ends. When a show closes, the musicians are subsequently unemployed and must seek another show through MCs. Additionally, Broadway musicals typically do not benefit from longevity like other employment relationships. For example, as opposed to well-known statistical anomalies, like "Cats" (18 years), most musicals remain open less than six months. Therefore, the musicians are regularly compelled to seek other employment whether on Broadway or not. It is precisely the subsequent rehiring that is the issue at hand. Although these hiring patterns are somewhat particular to Broadway musicians, an understanding of the musicians' situation could encourage other researchers/activists to investigate decision making in their own hiring practices.[50]

As discussed in the previous chapter, Broadway musicians must maintain a tractable relationship with the MC or their future employment is doubtful. Beyond previous encounters with a musician, the MCs decision on which musician to hire for a particular show is frequently influenced by gossip, rumors, and innuendo. Although an MC might disagree, I have directly witnessed and interviewed musicians who have witnessed what can be considered arbitrary and capricious hiring decisions made by MCs. In essence, MCs hold powerful positions vis-à-vis Broadway musicians because these 4 sometimes 5, individuals hire all of the musicians who play in Broadway theatres.[51]

What is seemingly more difficult than maintaining a good relationship with the MC is the commencement of such a relationship. Currently over 1200 musicians are considered Broadway musicians,[52] but many more aspire to hold these positions. As one musician writes:

> ... I have been trying to contact [MC] Mr. Miller for over five years and have never received even an impolite "thanks but no thanks" from him. I have tried e-mail, phone calls and regular mail to no avail. I am told he uses the same seven people over and over and over again. (Atkins)

MCs do not typically hold auditions, rather they usually hire and rehire musicians who they know personally or hire musicians who are recommended by other musicians. Indeed, in a January 2005 in Local 802's newspaper the *Allegro*, John Miller the most prolific MC reiterated this point. The point is that it is not only difficult for musicians to get rehired, but it is also extremely onerous to obtain an initial position.

Broadway musicians, therefore, tend to covet their positions because of the obstacles involved in being hired and rehired by the MC. Because of their fear of retaliation by the MC, the result is a strenuous resistance to change or any kind of boat rocking by the musicians. To the musicians' detriment, any discussions concerning hiring practices do not occur, and therefore, neither Local 802 officials nor the musicians challenge these procedures. This fragile situation is precisely the central element of the proposed prototype in the next chapter.

E. CONCLUSION

The object of the discussion in this chapter was to uncover the similarities between Broadway musicians' concerns and those of workers in other industries so that researchers and worker advocates might gain insight as to how they might scrutinize their own situation and possibly implement the suggestions that will be offered in Chapter 4. The basic strategies employed by Local 802 to improve the musicians' working conditions are to increase and sustain open communication with the musicians, to ensure the anonymity of grieving musicians, and to encourage a united front as a union vis-à-vis management. The result of these strategies has been mixed. The union has been successful in achieving increases in the real wage package; however, at the same time, it has been unsuccessful in achieving significant improvements in job security, reducing the Producers' dependence on the use of electronic labor saving devices, and implementing health and safety restrictions. A musician cannot be fired without "just cause" while working on a particular musical, but if for some reason a musician has problems with the MC, s/he risks not being hired for a future show. Furthermore, the many safety and health concerns of the musicians have been either ignored completely or only disingenuously addressed by the Producers. When Local 802, like other unions and their commentators, focuses its attention on the crisis *du jour*, it is "applying palliatives, not curing the malady" (Marx, *Value* 61). More successes might be achieved with a class-transformative agenda, and thus it might be advantageous for Local 802 to maintain its current efforts and strategies in tandem with a class-transformative agenda. If, for example, the union were somehow able to assist in transforming the capitalist class positions the musicians currently hold to communist class positions, not only might the musicians achieve more successes, they would also eradicate their own exploitation. This issue will be further explored and detailed in the following chapter.

4 Class Transformation

A. INTRODUCTION

The previous chapter explained how the Broadway musicians, while in a somewhat unique situation, have issues and problems similar to those of other workers. Addressing their concerns, like most other trade union officials, Local 802 is reactive rather than proactive. That is, unions tend to address problems as they occur and often resolve them temporarily with little or no prolonged vision or strategic plan. Typically, unions prioritize wage and benefits improvements, and although this is paramount to improving workers' lives, such an agenda falls short of being revolutionary.[1] Unions do not pursue revolutionary plans for various reasons such as budget constraints, lack of member participation, fear of the unknown, and opposition to radicalism (Bacon). However, a central component to a long-range strategic plan is a comprehensive investigation into workers' specific situation and a clear understanding of their class position(s) vis-à-vis their employers.

This chapter commences with a succinct discussion of New Marxian Class Analysis (NMCA).[2] NMCA helps to clarify the Broadway musicians' and their constituents' class positions, and the implications such positions imply for both short and long term strategies. Considering the musicians in this particular manner reveals the possibility of a radical change in their working lives. Therefore, as a viable option for the musicians, a specific prototype is proposed that will give them an opportunity for a revolutionary change in their class position and might yield improvements in their working conditions and possibly address some of the issues/concerns raised in the previous chapter. The final section of this chapter is a description of the post-class transformation relationships the Broadway musicians might encounter with the various constituencies: the union, the Producers, the Music Coordinators, the theatre owners, the conductors, and even amongst themselves. In the conclusion, a rationale is then provided which establishes that this type of change is indeed achievable in modern society.

B. NEW MARXIAN CLASS ANALYSIS METHODOLOGY

> Marxian class analysis is then the theorization of the overdetermina-
> tion of that social process, that is, its interaction with all other process
> that comprise its conditions of existence. (Resnick and Wolff, *Knowl-
> edge* 111)

The methodology of NMCA is chosen to investigate and to suggest possible
remedies and improvements via a class structure change of the Broadway
musicians. NMCA is preferred because it offers a plethora of options to the
researcher regarding how to improve workers' lives using class as its entry
point. Class, as used in this book "is understood as a distinct social process . . . it is the economic process of performing and appropriating surplus
labor" (26).[3] Because NMCA uses *class* as its entry point, when analyzing
the production process itself, the researcher can uncover how social structures might be changed to improve workers' situations. It gets to the core
of the basic work relationship by developing a network of events and processes that form the environment in which workers toil. Unlike other types
Marxian analyses that focus on power over or ownership of the means of
production, within the NMCA framework, the various agents' class positions are defined by their relationship to the surplus produced, and the particular agents' positions are defined by who produces, appropriates, and/or
distributes the surplus value. "A class analysis in this sense *classifies* individuals in a society in terms of their relationship to this surplus" (Resnick
and Wolff, *Class Theory* 8). In capitalism, the producers of the surplus do
not participate in its appropriation and distribution processes; for example,
workers produce surplus value, which is subsequently appropriated and distributed by the capitalists. Conversely, in communism, the surplus producers themselves appropriate and distribute any surplus produced.[4] Because
capitalist workers do not appropriate the surplus they produce, they are
exploited. In opposition, communist workers, who appropriate their own
surplus, are not exploited. The primary focus of this book and the prototype offered below is the eradication of exploitation because exploitation
is the social theft of the fruits of workers' labor. Moreover, working conditions might be improved within communism, which often have failed
within capitalism. Finally, the mere notion of a communist agenda might
improve working conditions within capitalism, because simply the threat to
capitalists' loss of control over the surplus might be just enough incentive to
take necessary steps to appease the workers at least in the short run.

NMCA makes the distinction between two discrete class processes,
the fundamental and the subsumed. In the former, surplus is produced
and appropriated; in the latter, surplus is subsequently distributed and
received. Thus, within the capitalist class structure, workers hold the

fundamental class position of surplus value producers, and capitalists hold the fundamental class position of surplus value appropriators, while simultaneously holding the subsumed class position of surplus distributor. Capitalists make payments in the form of wages to workers for their fundamental class position as surplus value producer, but the wages paid is only for the workers necessary labor, or "the quantity of labor time necessary to produce the consumables customarily required by the direct producer to keep working" (Resnick and Wolff, *Knowledge* 115). No payment is made for the surplus labor produced by capitalist workers, that is the workers receive no payment for extra time they toil over their necessary labor time. Capitalists occupy a subsumed class position as surplus value distributors and therefore subsequently make distributions that secure their conditions of existence as capitalists. That is, the capitalist must make these payments to retain their fundamental class position as surplus value appropriator. Subsumed class payments may take a variety of different forms, such as profits to the capitalists, managers' salaries, dividends to stockholders, royalties, or taxes, among an extensive variety of other possible payments.[5] In contrast, in a communist class process workers hold both fundamental class positions (producer and appropriator of surplus) as well as the subsumed class position of distributor, thus giving communist workers control over the fruits of their labor, that is, the distributors of the surplus they produced.

When someone other than its direct producers extracts the surplus produced, exploitation is present. Therefore, capitalism is exploitative because the capitalists seize the surplus produced by the workers, and therefore it is the capitalists who make surplus distributions, not those producing it. Bear in mind that, capitalist workers, those who create the surplus, receive no payments for the surplus labor they produce—any benefits from the surplus go directly to the capitalist. A preferred workers' position would be one devoid of exploitation, such as would be the condition within communism. "A communist class structure exists if and when the people who collectively produce a surplus are likewise and identically the people who collectively receive and distribute it" (Resnick and Wolff, *Class Theory* 9). Accordingly, a revolutionary, class transformative strategy would facilitate the removal of the capitalist's fundamental class position as the appropriator of surplus value so that the surplus value producers (workers) hold this position. Unions can facilitate this process, but for the most part have not pursued such an agenda, the failure of trade unions according to Marx.

A class analysis of a specific site of production thus illustrates how a union might facilitate such a class transformation. The following is an NMCA class analysis of the Broadway musicians. This analysis reveals the specific fundamental, subsumed, and non-class positions that Broadway musicians and their constituents occupy which permits the reader to clearly comprehend Broadway musicians' particular working circumstances and subsequently their class positions. Also provided is an investigation into the components of the Broadway musicians' wage package, this is provided to demonstrate not only potential areas of solidarity amongst the musicians, but also to underscore potential areas of debate and struggle amongst themselves. Furthermore, the class analysis also exposes possible points where subtle changes in the musicians' employment situation(s) may indeed radically change the circumstances in which they toil daily.

C. CLASS ANALYSIS AND THE BROADWAY MUSICIANS

> [I]n a capitalist class structure . . . different individuals typically occupy the two fundamental class positions: one group performs the surplus labor while a different group appropriates the surplus. (Resnick and Wolff, *Class Theory* 14)

Often musicians are not recognized as workers, they are often thought of as non-productive workers, or simply entertainers, indeed when one speaks of the process of performing music, the term 'play' is used and the musicians are referred to as players, not workers as in most industries. Joseph Weber, the first president of the American Federation of Musicians, knew differently, he had an unambiguous grasp of a musician's role within capitalism. In 1895 he exclaimed in a speech to musicians:

> We musicians are employed under the same conditions of any other workers . . . We may be artists, but we still work for wages . . . [We] are exploited by our employers in the same manner as any other wage-earners who stand alone. Therefore we must organize, cooperate and become active in the economic field like other workers. (Zinn, et al. 126)

Indeed, the Broadway musicians are like other capitalist workers who sell the commodity, labor power for a wage. The capitalists in this instance, the Musicals' Producers purchase labor power from workers by hiring musicians for their ability to perform live music in exchange for a payment, their wage. Any productive capitalist has the expectation that in return for paying wages to workers, s/he will receive more than original value of the labor power s/he has purchased, that is, a surplus will be created by the workers and collected by the capitalists. As such, Broadway Producers anticipate that the musicians will produce a new commodity, music for a Broadway Production that is more valuable than the wages paid by the Producers. The difference between the wage (the value of the labor power) and the value added by the workers to the new commodity music for a Broadway show is the surplus value, for which musicians are currently not compensated. The Producers directly appropriate the surplus value and make various distributions that secure their conditions of existence as capitalists.[6] What follows is an analysis of the case of Broadway musicians that uses the NCMA to understanding the distinctive relationships between the musicians and their constituents.

1. Fundamental Class Positions, Payments, and Revenues

According to Resnick and Wolff, a New Marxian class analysis:

> *[C]lassifies* individuals in a society in terms of their relationship to this surplus. It asks who performs the necessary plus surplus labor, how is this socially organized, and how does the organization of the surplus impact the larger society? Secondly a class analysis asks who first receives the surplus from the laborers, to whom do these receivers then distribute it, for what purposes, and how do these distributions affect the larger society? The analysis is particularly concerned with whether it is the same or different groups of people who respectively perform, appropriate and/ or receive distributions of the surplus. (*Class Theory* 8)

The first task then is to explore the musicians' relationship to the surplus. As discussed above, the Broadway musicians are hired by MCs, who themselves are the Producers, direct employees. The musicians sell their labor power to the Producer who immediately consumes it during a musical production.[7] As discussed in Chapter 2, the Producer qua managing member of the LLC, is the capitalist who immediately and directly appropriates any surplus value produced by the musicians (as well as other productive[8] workers on Broadway). S/he is the direct recipient of the 'gross' box office receipts and has the absolute authority to make distributions as s/he wishes or is legally and culturally bound. Thus, the Producer is indeed the productive capitalist and holds the fundamental class position of surplus value appropriator because of his/her position as the direct (immediate) recipient of the gross receipts. Concurrently, the Producer also holds the subsumed class position as distributor of the surplus value.[9] First, however, the fundamental class process, payments, and revenues that s/he must make to secure his/her conditions of existence as capitalist must be examined to uncover possible opportunities to usurp the capitalist's fundamental class position as surplus value appropriator with the goal of having the Broadway musicians themselves occupy this role.

Although the relationship between the musicians and the Producer is complex and obscured by legal titles and hiring procedures, the Producer is indubitably the first recipient (appropriator) of the surplus labor produced by the musicians as well as some of the musical's other workers such as the actors.[10] The musicians do not appropriate nor distribute the surplus value they produce; the Producer holds this position. Musicians are, however, free to sell their labor power to whomever they choose because they are not contractually, emotionally, physically, legally, or culturally obliged to only provide their labor power to one Producer, that is they are neither serfs, nor slaves (Weiner, *Power Hitters*; Fraad, et al.); thus the capitalist class structure prevails on Broadway.

The Producer is the productive or "functioning" capitalist (Resnick and Wolff, *Knowledge* 141). S/he is "the 'individual' who exchanges a quantum of value for labor power plus means of production and receives back a larger quantum of value in produced commodities" (142). Because s/he is the initial recipient of the surplus value of which s/he did not him/herself produce, the Producer holds the fundamental class position of capitalist. Indeed, it is the Producer as the "managing member"[11] who holds both the legal and theoretical position of Broadway capitalist. Conversely, musicians occupy the fundamental class position as surplus value producers. Exploitation, the act of appropriating the surplus value by someone other than its producer, is unambiguous on Broadway, and the Broadway musicians are indeed exploited workers. In summary, the Broadway musicians are paid the socially necessary wage to produce a product that has more value than the wages they receive. The Broadway musicians receive no payment for the extra product (the surplus they produce); this is the precise definition of exploitation—production of surplus value with no recompense.

The Broadway musicians sell their labor power to the capitalist Producer via Music Coordinators (MCs). Until Disney appeared on Broadway in 1994, the Broadway participants generally refused to acknowledge capitalism's presence; in fact, there was an enduring illusion that the production of a Broadway musical is a collaborative/collective effort devoid of exploitation. Nonetheless, Broadway's class structure in terms of surplus, both pre- and post-Disney is indeed capitalist. Steeped in tradition, the Broadway participants, including the union and its officials, staff, and members do not challenge Broadway musicals' capitalist class structure and may even contribute to its continued existence. That is, they indeed provide some conditions of existence necessary for the capitalist class process.

The Producer establishes him/herself as the capitalist by ensuring the receipt of the surplus value produced by the productive workers. S/he does this by first acquiring a 'property' from the book-writer, lyrist, and composer. Subsequently, the Producer secures the productive[12] workers, such as the actors and the musicians. Although, these workers may not be hired directly by the Producer him/herself, the capitalist sets in motion their employment, whether through an MC, agent, or whomever. The 'property' (the musical) is one of the means of production, and as such the capitalist makes payments[13] to the 'property' owner(s) for access to it. The payment for this property may or may not be an upfront cash payment to the book-writer, lyrist, and composer. Moreover, this payment may be zero because the book-writer, lyrist, and composer may opt to forfeit any advance payment in lieu of a possible larger future payment in the form of a royalty based on the show's success. A royalty is a payment from the appropriated surplus value, thus it a subsumed class payment. If no surplus value is realized, then indeed the payment for the 'property' is indeed zero.

A. Broadway Musicians' Wages Part I

While it is necessary for the capitalist to secure access to the means of production, in this case the 'property,' in order for there to be a musical, simply acquiring or having access to this is not sufficient for the creation of a Broadway musical. The productive workers transform the means of production into a new commodity, and the productive workers are integral[14] in the production process. Without productive workers no new, more valuable commodity can be produced. For his or her fundamental class position as surplus value producing worker, each musician (as well as other productive workers such as actors) receives a minimum[15] scale wage package.[16] This wage for the Broadway side-musicians includes their basic scale wage, currently[17] $1500.75 per week for eight shows, 6.125% vacation payment, 5% pension,[18] $58 per week for health benefits, and other assorted premiums for producing surplus value. For example, if a musician plays more than one 'non-related' instrument s/he is said to be 'doubling' and is paid a premium of 12.5% for the first double, 6.25% for each double thereafter. Thus this premium is often paid by the Producers because the musician playing the additional instrument rather than not playing at any particular instance is producing more surplus value s/he would otherwise with only one instrument (League, *Collective Bargaining Agreement* 19).[19] That is, the double premium is paid because another musician does not need to be hired; therefore one musician does the work of two or possibly more. Broadway musicians also receive overtime premiums for shows that last longer than three hours, for a third show on the same day, and the second show on Sundays.[20] This wage is the payment the Broadway musicians receive in exchange for the sale of their commodity, labor power (Resnick and Wolff, *Knowledge* 151).

Conductors receive an additional 75% above minimum scale wages for their role as orchestra leaders. Leading an orchestra, as the conductor does, is a fundamental class position because it is a surplus value producing endeavor. Marx, in *Capital, Volume 3* makes it clear that the conductor's position as a leader of the production process is indeed productive of surplus value, and therefore, the conductor holds the fundamental class position like the side-musicians. Marx states:

> . . . in all labour where many individuals cooperate, the interconnection and unity of the process is necessarily represented in a governing will, and in functions that concern not the detailed work but rather the workplace and its activity as a whole, as with the conductor of an orchestra. This is productive labour that has to be performed in any combined mode of production. (507)

Because of the collective bargaining agreement with Local 802, the capitalist Producer is contractually obligated to make these wage payments to each working musician.[21] Musicians may indeed receive additional payments for services beyond the fundamental class process of performing music that they provide the Producer; however, these are in the form of subsumed and non-class payments which will be discussed below. Thus, to summarize, the Broadway musicians and the conductors in their role as orchestra leaders occupy the fundamental class position as surplus value producers because they sell the commodity labor power to a Broadway Producer. For this service, the musicians receive a payment in the form of their wage package and they receive no payment for the surplus value they produce. The capitalist Producer holds the fundamental class position of appropriator of the surplus value because s/he immediately appropriates the surplus value and distributes to various constituents to secure his/her conditions of existence as capitalist.

2. Subsumed Class Positions, Payments, and Revenues

> Marx stresses repeatedly that occupants of subsumed class positions may either be employees of industrial capitalists or alternatively direct their own independent enterprises. (Resnick and Wolff, *Knowledge* 134)

Besides their fundamental class position as surplus value appropriators, Producers are distributors of surplus value; they make surplus value distributions to various entities to maintain their positions as capitalists.[22] It is important to understand some of these payments because it allows the researcher the scope to uncover specific instances that might allow for radical or possibly even quite subtle changes that might drastically alter the workers' situations. Producers make a variety of subsumed class payments to a variety of individuals and institutions: to theatre owners in the form of rent for access to private property, to the State in form of taxes so that they may continue doing business, to composers and writers in the form of royalties so that they may have access to the 'property' they have created, to the League in the form of membership dues for representation in grievances and negotiations as well as other benefits such as advertising the League may provide, and to Music Coordinators in the form of weekly salaries for the provision of a Broadway orchestra.[23] Each of these payments is ostensibly necessary to secure the Producer's position as capitalist.

These payments are necessary and minimizing these payments is, or at least should be, a primary objective of the capitalist. Therefore, the capitalist Producer and surplus value recipients continually struggle over the amount of said payments. Furthermore, although such disputes sometimes are over minor details, this does not preclude their relative importance. For example, musicals must have a venue, and therefore, rent, a subsumed class payment, must be paid to the theatre owners. Producers and the theatre owners may disagree on the length of the rental or the amount of rent to be paid, but in the end, the capitalist Producer has a choice of only 32 Broadway theatres, which are all owned by three for-profit organizations, the Nederlander, the Jujamcyn, and the Schubert. It is a formidable oligopoly which until recently was impenetrable. It took the two giant enterprises in the theatrical industry, Disney and Clear Channel, to challenge the oligopolistic barrier. The two theatres owned by Disney and Clear Channel only house their own Productions, that is they are currently not rented to external Production companies.

Another example of a struggle over a surplus value distribution is one between the Producer and the writers/composers. In order for a Production to happen at all, there must be an end product to sell; therefore, the Producer must have purchased the musical from the person who wrote dialogue and/or composed the music. There may be a dispute over the amount of the upfront payment or the backend royalty, and there might be a lesser payment to a new author/composer than a more established one. Whether the Producer pays for the musical upfront, backend, or some sort of a combination of the two, obtaining the 'product' is absolutely necessary. The writers/composers relative power, prestige, experience, notoriety, talent, etc. significantly influences the amount of the subsumed class payments. For example, the quintessential singer/songwriter Elton John composed the music for "Lion King" therefore Disney made a subsumed class payment to Mr. John that would probably exceed any payment to an unknown or inexperienced composer. The important issue is that the Producers must make subsumed class payments to writers and composers, the size of which is the impetus of struggle.

As stated above, the Producers also make subsumed class payments to MCs for their service of providing an orchestra for a Broadway Musical Production. The MCs often not only receive a weekly paycheck for the entire length of the show, they may also receive royalties, and health and pension benefits. Moreover, because the MCs are members of Local 802, the pension and health benefits paid by the Producers on their behalf are made to the respective Local 802 union pension and health plans. This complication aside, the payment for services of the MC is a subsumed class payment, a direct distribution of the surplus value. And as will be seen below, the MC's payment becomes superfluous under a new class structure that will be offered below. Nonetheless, in the current situation, MCs make every attempt to secure the greatest payment for their services. Ultimately, however, the capitalist makes all of the payments mentioned here because he believes it secures his conditions of existence as appropriator/distributor of surplus value—in other words, as a productive capitalist.

A. Broadway Musicians' Wages Part II

The Producers also make additional payments to the Broadway musicians and conductors in the form of recompense that exceeds the basic minimum scale wages and benefits. That is, musicians' wages not only include payments for necessary labor for their role as surplus value producers, they might also occupy subsumed class positions and may receive additional income for occupying such positions. For instance every Broadway musician must belong to the union, Local 802, consequently it might be argued that the musicians monopolize the supply of labor and, therefore, receive a wage higher than socially necessary because of the Union wage effect.[24] Unlike most other unions, Local 802 does not negotiate maximum wages or equal wages for the musicians, only minimum scale wages.

Indeed, musicians may negotiate a wage over the minimum scale wage. Article III.G. of the collective bargaining agreement states that: "[n]othing in this [collective bargaining agreement] shall prevent any individual from negotiating a wage in excess of the minimum wage"(League, *Collective Bargaining Agreement* 6).[25] Skills, talent, experience, and even nepotism are but some of the many reasons a Producer might agree to pay over the minimum. In any case, this payment is above the socially necessary, or scale wage. Over scale payments are not common, but on the rare occasion when they do occur, they tend to be met with enmity by the other musicians. Local 802, the Producers, and the musicians themselves have not attempted to change this clause, and a future reconsideration is highly unlikely. When questioned about this, Bill Moriarity, President of Local 802, stated that each (most) musician believes that s/he is worthy of over-scale payments and, therefore, believes that s/he will someday be a recipient of such a payment, however unlikely, and that it would be damaging politically to address changing it (Moriarity, *Interview*).

Besides over-scale payments, some Broadway musicians benefit from a variety of subsumed class distributions, which during the 1998 negotiations the Producers proposed to either reduce or eliminate. Typically, capitalists make surplus value distributions to the occupants of subsumed class positions in order to secure their conditions of existence as surplus value appropriators, and payments that do not have this function are superfluous, so any respectable profit maximizing capitalist would seek to reduce or eliminate them in part or completely, which is exactly what the Producers attempted during the 1998 negotiations. The Producers' quest was to minimize some of the payments to Broadway musicians and conductors, thereby revealing that the capitalists no longer believed that certain payments were necessary to secure their conditions of existence. Before the 1998 collective bargaining agreement was signed, a extra percentage of the musicians' base salary were made to Librarians (12.5%), First Trumpet ($75/week), Associate Conductors (30%), and Designated Contractors (50%) for these subsumed class positions. During the 1998 negotiations, the Producers comprehensively attacked almost every subsumed class position held by Broadway musicians so that the surplus value distribution for these positions might be eliminated.[26]

Most collective bargaining agreements have idiosyncratic clauses, and on the face might look either innocuous or imprudent. Unless one understands the history this certainly includes some of premium payments in the Broadway musicians' collective bargaining agreement. For example, the librarian premium of 12.5% was a quasi-political patronage payment occasionally given to a friend of the MC or, sometimes, a senior musician who did not have access to other premiums, such as doubling. The responsibilities of the Librarian are negligible in that his/her basic task was to put the music on the music stands prior to the beginning of each performance. This responsibility, however, waned after the official opening of the show. While a show is in previews, which may range from two to four weeks, changes are made to the score and require the sheet music to be gathered, revised, and then put back on the stands before the next preview performance. Subsequent to the official opening, modifications to the score are seldom made, thereby making the Librarian's responsibilities inconsequential. Nevertheless, the Librarian would receive a premium of 12.5% for the run of the show. The Producers/capitalists understood that the Librarians' function was not required and not a necessary condition of existence that secured their position as capitalists, so they fervently argued to eliminate this payment. The Producers succeeded in eradicating the Librarian premium subsequent to opening, and now it is only paid on the rare occasion that the Librarian actually performs duties in that capacity.

The Producers were not successful, however, in their pursuit to eliminate or reduce payments for doubling, first trumpet, seventh consecutive day, second show on Sunday, or a third performance in a day; those premiums, although not essential to secure the condition of existence of capitalist reproduction remain unchanged in the collective bargaining agreement. They did prevail, however, in renegotiating the premium payment to the associate conductors for this subsumed class position. Prior to the 1998 contract, associate conductors received a 30% wage premium for all hours s/he worked (League, *Collective Bargaining Agreement* 5.[27] Although the conductor generally chooses his/her associate, s/he is hired by the MC and is officially an employee of the theatre owner, as are the side-musicians. The associate conductor's primary function is to replace the conductor if s/he falls ill or cannot perform his/her conductor duties at a performance and/or rehearsal. The associate conductor does not do anything more than a side-musician, but when needed, s/he must have the knowledge and skill to perform the duties of the conductor. If the primary conductor schedules his/her absence, the associate conductor would then assume the role of conductor and be paid the conductor's premium of 75%. Another orchestra member would then receive the 30% associate conductor premium. During every performance prior to the 1998 contract, there was a conductor receiving a premium of 75% and an associate conductor receiving a premium of 30%.

The associate conductor's premium is different than the premium payment made to the conductor for his/her position in the fundamental class process of surplus value production. The associate conductor's premium is a subsumed class payment because s/he simply performed as a side-musician and received the payment only because it was a contractual obligation.

During the 1998 negotiations, the Producers did not seek to eliminate the associate conductor's position, nor the premium paid to the associate. However, they did attempt to reduce the burden of always paying this premium.[28] The Producers were unsuccessful in eliminating any payment to another orchestra member who was 'moved up' to the associate's position during performances; they were successful however, in changing the terms of the collective bargaining agreement to reduce the associate conductor's premium payment during certain rehearsal situations. The result is a decrease in the surplus distributions made to the Broadway musicians by the capitalist Producers.

Even though the League's proposal to discontinue the requirement of the Designated Contractor's[29] position was also unsuccessful, an interesting discussion emanated from the proposal. The collective bargaining agreement requires that the Designated Contractor be a playing member of the orchestra. His/her primary functions, for which s/he receives a 50% wage premium, are those of a personnel manger: they maintain daily records, keep attendance, provide payroll information, and so forth. In NMCA terms, the Designated Contractor holds the subsumed class position as personnel manager for which s/he receives an additional 50% wage. The Producers' central argument was that they should have the right to hire personnel manager(s) of their choice and that this manager should not necessarily be a playing musician in the show. Furthermore, the collective bargaining agreement states in Article II.A. (1) "Hiring Practices" that:

> The Employers shall engage all musicians required by them through Contractors, as heretofore. The Contractor for each show shall be selected by the Producer and Theatre Owner in consultation with Local 802. The Executive Board of Local 802 shall be immediately notified of each such selection and all such selections shall be subject to review by the Executive Board of Local 802 for the sole purpose of determining whether the Contractor has engaged in any conduct inimical to Local 802. The Contractor shall be a playing musician in the orchestra for the run of the show. (League, *Collective Bargaining Agreement* 3)

So, the Producers also contended that Designated Contractors do not assume the hiring responsibilities spelled out in the collective bargaining agreement.

It would appear from a cursory reading of the collective bargaining agreement that a playing member of the orchestra and a union member should be the person who hires musicians for Broadway shows. This is not, nor has ever been, the practice on Broadway. Historically the MCs were playing musicians in the Broadway orchestras, they were hired by the theatre owners to amass and employ the orchestra for that particular theatre.[30] Due to the various transformations of the Broadway collective bargaining agreement over (approximately) the past 50 years, as discussed above, the musicians are no longer engaged by a specific theatre owner for 'house' orchestras; they are now engaged by a specific musical, but they remain as official employees of the theatre owners. During the period of 'house' orchestra, each 'house,' or theatre, had its own Music Contractor/ Coordinator and he played in that orchestra. With the end of the practice of using 'house' orchestras in 1964, the Producers continued to look to the MCs to hire orchestras for their particular musicals and the MCs continued to play in the orchestra. Eventually, the Producers preferred hiring the same MC for various shows, and what evolved are the hiring practices that exist on Broadway today.

The MC hires an orchestra, and then he assigns one musician to the job as the Designated Contractor, who receives a 50% subsumed class payment for this extra responsibility. For his role as the hirer and manager of the orchestra, the MC receives a subsumed class payment for this function as 'labor broker.' Something a bit idiosyncratic is the fact that the MC might himself occupy the fundamental class position as a wage-earning surplus value producing playing musician. Moreover, the same MC may also occupy the subsumed class position as the Designated Contractor who receives a surplus value distribution of 50% of scale wages for this function. On the other hand, it is explicitly stated in the collective bargaining agreement that the Designated Contractor may not occupy the position of conductor, associate conductor, or librarian. That is, if for example the MC chooses to be the orchestra's conductor, he may not deem himself the Designated Contractor.

Although the Producers distribute other subsumed class payments to secure their conditions of existence as surplus value appropriators, the discussion above is meant to reveal sources of struggle over these payments directly concerned with the Broadway musicians. All of the subsumed class payments are a portion of the surplus value produced by other—in this case, the musicians.[31] The surplus value produced by the musicians enables payments to many entities, including their own controller, the Music Coordinator. That is, the musicians reinforce their own exploitation due to their very position as surplus value producers sans appropriators. To eliminate their exploitive positions, the Broadway musicians themselves need to become the appropriators of the surplus they produce.

3. Non-Class Payments, Positions, and Revenues

Besides their fundamental and subsumed class positions, the Producers as well as the musicians occupy non-class positions, of which payments are made and revenues are realized for occupying such positions. Most notably, the Producers hold the non-class position of buyer of the commodity labor power, and the Broadway musicians hold the non-class position as seller of labor power. In addition to these non-class positions, the Producers and Broadway musicians could receive or make non-class payments. A nonclass revenue for the Producer may be obtained by the sale of concessions in theatre lobbies. In each Broadway musical there are concession stands that sell candy, beverages, and show paraphernalia including T-shirts, posters, and cast albums, the profits of which go directly to the Producer. The workers selling these products are only involved with a commodity exchange; they are not producing the goods. That is, surplus value is not produced at this moment. Therefore, this relationship is one of exchange, that is no new, more valuable commodity is being produced by the sale of such concessions. Thus this is a non-class exchange process.

A. Broadway Musicians' Wages Part III

The Broadway musicians also occupy non-class positions while in their capacity as such. Obtaining an orchestra member position on Broadway is not only very competitive, it is impossible without access to a MC. That is, the MC restricts the supply of positions. As such, working Broadway musicians might need to make a payment to the MC, i.e. the 'labor broker' to retain his/her position on Broadway. "A nonclass payment may flow from laborers to 'parasites between the capitalists and the wage-labourer' engage in the 'subletting of labour'" (Resnick and Wolff, *Knowledge* 153). I have no knowledge of MCs actually collecting payments directly from the Broadway musicians for access to jobs. However, this payment might not be in dollars, but in time. A particular MC may require the musicians to come to the theatre a half hour before the downbeat; meanwhile the musicians contractually scheduled start time is only that they be in place for the downbeat. Thus the musician is making a nonclass payment of a half hour of his/her time because s/he must keep a tractable relationship with the MC for future employment opportunities.[32]

The musicians might also make nonclass payments to psychotherapists, acupuncturists, or message therapists because of the stress they undergo trying to maintain a working relationship with the MC. Many musicians have complained to me that this is indeed the case; therefore, while the MC receives no additional payment from the musician; the musician does indeed incur an additional expense for his/her own job security.

As mentioned in Chapter 2, there are currently approximately 6200 musicians that Local 802 deems Broadway musicians. At any given time, the greatest number of positions on Broadway has not exceeded 325, that is, there are approximately 20 musicians vying for but one position. Moreover, there are many more musicians who would like to 'break in' on Broadway but have not been able to secure an interview or audition with one of the MCs, thus the MC restricts access to these coveted positions from many other musicians. For example, one musician, Richard Atkins, a veteran with 30 years experience has been attempting to contact MC John Miller via various means, such as phone calls, US mail, and emails. Mr. Atkins correspondences have gone unanswered by Mr. Miller—prompting Mr. Atkins to question the entire Broadway hiring procedure in a letter to Local 802's newsletter, the *Allegro*. The important aspect of these issues are twofold: if the MC is the gatekeeper to Broadway jobs as such, the musicians make nonclass payments to secure that the MC will hire them in the future; therefore the Broadway musicians' wages are less than what they would be under other circumstances. That is, the wage is less than the value of the Broadway musicians' labor power. In essence, the Broadway musicians give a "rebate" to the MCs, a non-class payment for access to the job (Resnick and Wolff, *Knowledge* 153).

What has been shown here is that wages are not simply payments for work performed or surplus value produced; that simply because the Broadway musicians' wages earn a contracted wage does not necessarily lend itself to a level of solidarity that many union pundits profess. That is, just being a wage-earning musician does not necessarily translate into unity. The delineation of wages received is therefore an integral mechanism that will be valuable in the future discussion regarding class transformation because the differentiation of wages by task is a cause of difference.

The Broadway musicians receive or make payments for their work in the orchestra. The Broadway musicians' total wage (W_{total}) has various components and is comprised of fundamental, subsumed, and non-class payments. They receive the socially necessary wages for the value of the labor power for the production of surplus value (W_1). Some Broadway musicians receive subsumed class payments for over-scale or holding the subsumed class positions of either librarian or designated contractor (W_2). Furthermore, the wage received may be reduced due to payments to the MC for access to the job, a nonclass payment (W_3). Therefore, the Broadway musicians' wage equation is:

$$W_{total} = W_1 + W_2 + W_3$$

where $W_1 > 0,$[33] $W_2 > 0$, and $W_3 < 0$.

It is important to delineate the various components of wages received by the Broadway musicians because potential internal struggles by the musicians and Local 802 are revealed at this time. For example, a musician who continually receives over-scale wages might resist any change by Local 802 that might eliminate or make modification to these payments. Currently, only managers make the decisions about which musicians receive over-scale payments; that is, there is no democratic or contractual process regarding the provision of over-scale payments.[34] Recall that the Broadway musicians do not want to eliminate such payments, in that most of them believe that they too will be the recipients of such payments in the future.[35] The point is that by using the NMCA framework potential areas of controversy can be revealed prior to implementation of any proposed changes in class structure. Therefore, the musicians in this case would have the opportunity to solicit input from fellow members regarding the issues at stake rather than supporting their own capitalist exploitation.

Though the Broadway musicians receive wage payments from the surplus, and therefore hold subsumed class positions as a surplus value recipients, the musicians remain the workers who produce that very surplus value they receive. The issue at hand, however, is that it is not the musicians themselves who make the decision on how the surplus value is distributed. Of course, some of the capitalist's payments are explicitly in the collective bargaining agreement, thus the musicians through Local 802 participate at some level on the surplus value distributions. Because of the Broadway musicians' role as surplus value producers with no associated role as surplus value appropriators and distributors, the Broadway musicians are exploited in the Marxian sense. It is this very issue of exploitation elimination that is paramount. As will be shown below, eradication of exploitation will offer more opportunities to the musicians, it will radically alter the terms under which they daily toil.

D. CLASS TRANSFORMATION PROTOTYPE

Exploitation is objectionable, particularly to Marxists who believe that workers should appropriate the surplus value they produce. Nonetheless, in the United States the socially accepted economic structure is capitalism and the issue of exploitation is veiled by notions of economic freedom propagated by those who do not include notions of exploitation in their rhetoric.[36] In a predominately capitalist wage economy as in the US, workers are alienated from the fruits of their labor, and thus exploitation is guaranteed. Unions have a role in exposing capitalism for what it is and take action to make the appropriate and/or necessary changes to a class structure that does not 'steal' the fruits of their labor from the workers. A non-alienating class structure that includes collective appropriation by the surplus producers is the preferred alternative—collective surplus appropriation is the precise New Marxian definition of communism.[37] Without a collective/communist class structure exploitation persists and, therefore, has a tendency to exacerbate specific problems workers might needlessly endure. As I have shown, workers persist in supporting the wage differentials that consequently reinforce their own exploitation.

The act of someone taking the surplus value from those who produce it is social theft; however, given the dominant discourses and the acceptance of the capitalist class process as something to be revered, the whole notion of exploitation is obscured because of the political, social and economic conditions of existence under which capitalist workers toil. The Broadway musicians are not excluded from an entrenched level of ignorance; however, they are steeped in tradition and do not willingly accept change. More profound than just not accepting change, the musicians see themselves as part of the creative process and often they believe they participate in the decisions and, therefore, the success of the production. They often ignore problems, contract violations, or controversy for the good of the show. For example, as discussed in Chapter 3, the musicians at the Broadway production of "Beauty and the Beast" have long endured being inundated with the inhalation of poisonous and harmful particulates and gases that are emitted during the course of the show, and subsequently many have experienced serious health problems. The musicians, as well as all the other participants, willingly accept their established roles and class positions; that is, there has been no attempt to, nor has there even been a discussion of, changing class positions. Indeed, during many pre-collective bargaining meetings of the rank and file Theatre Committee, comments or questions about artistic, creative, political, or economic participation were summarily dismissed by union officials as out of their sphere of influence.

In the present view the Broadway musicians hold the fundamental class position of surplus value producer, and the Producers hold both the fundamental class position of surplus value appropriators and the subsumed class position of surplus value distributors. Thus the class structure of Broadway Musicals is indeed capitalist. The capitalists pay a wage to the Broadway musicians for their necessary labor, any amount above that wage is the surplus produced by the musicians. Exploitation is palpable on Broadway because the capitalist Producers immediately and directly appropriate the surplus value produced by the musicians. The musicians have absolutely no voice or influence regarding how the surplus is distributed; only the Producers do. If a transformative change in class structure from capitalism to communism could be achieved, the musicians' working conditions might be drastically altered. The prototype presented here is an example of how the Broadway musicians might achieve the revolutionary change from capitalism to communism.

Since the objective of a class transformation is to eliminate exploitation, it is necessary to include a strategy to eliminate the Producer's fundamental class position of surplus value appropriator. The Broadway musicians could indeed liberate themselves from the role of exploited worker. For example, with guidance and assistance from Local 802, Broadway musicians could first form an orchestra with a conductor, prepare for a specific musical production, and then sell their services as a unit to the Producer. The Producer would supply the score, genre, and any other specific requirements to

Local 802. The union would then chose musicians with the skills, talent, and experience necessary for the Production to provide a quality product, presumably in a fair and democratic process.[38] In other words, the musicians would no longer sell their labor power to the Producer; instead, they would organize themselves into an independent collective entity and sell the services of that entity. In the proposed schema, the musicians would no longer hold the capitalist fundamental class position of surplus value producer. Instead they would hold the communist fundamental and subsumed class position of producers, appropriators, and distributors of the surplus. This subtle change would result in a class transformation from capitalism to communism, which would now mean that the musicians would make surplus distributions that could improve their working conditions,[39] rather than the current situation in which the Producer makes these decisions without regard for the workers. The Broadway musicians as a collective would both produce and appropriate the surplus embodied in the newly produced commodity music. Now the new commodity music is a communist commodity. The union could function as a facilitator of the change from capitalism to communism and, subsequently, as a facilitator of the new communist class process. The former exploiter, the Producer, would become the wholesale consumer, buying the services of a self-contained orchestra.

In the proposed arrangement, the orchestra would act as a collective, enjoying all the rights and privileges associated with such an arrangement. While there would be new obligations and costs, these could be addressed by the members of the orchestra under the aegis of Local 802. Additionally, the musicians would continue to remain Broadway musicians, performing the same job but under a radically different class configuration. In a post-transformation setting, the Broadway musicians would make decisions over the surplus, which they produce and now will make distributions of that surplus as the musicians see fit either by wish or by edict, not some other entity such as the Producers. For example, the musicians might make surplus distributions should they decide that an improved way of hiring members of a Broadway orchestra would be to hold auditions rather than employing the services of an MC. This could be done at Local 802 headquarters in the band room that can house at least one hundred musicians. Furthermore, the theatre committee or the membership at large could elect a panel of judges to implement the audition process. The Broadway musicians might choose some other process for access to jobs; the point is, however, that now the choice on how to do this would be the Broadway musicians', not the Producers'. The auditions could be either open to the public or only Local 802 members—however, membership might be required if the non-member is chosen for a musical. Either way, membership might increase in Local 802 because of its ability to restrict access to the coveted Broadway positions by non-members.

In summary, the musicians would move from the exploited class position of surplus value producer to the non-exploitative class position of both producer and appropriator of the surplus, while simultaneously seizing the producers' class position as surplus value appropriator (exploiter). The musicians' new relationship with the Producer is now one devoid of exploitation; its defining characteristic is exchange, a non-class process. The Producer would no longer make surplus distributions to secure his/her existence as capitalist vis-à-vis the musicians, because now the musicians would make surplus distributions that would secure their position as surplus producers, appropriators, and distributors. This would put the musicians in a situation where they might make improvements in their own work environments.

E. POST CLASS TRANSFORMATION AND THE BROADWAY PARTICIPANTS

1. The Broadway Musicians and Local 802

To some extent, the orchestra can act as an autonomous collective, and this should give the musicians more input in the work process. Under this modified organizational structure, the musicians no longer sell their labor power directly to the Producer. Instead, they sell their labor power as individuals to themselves as a collective. They will produce and sell, as a collective, a new communist commodity in the form of the services of an orchestra. The Broadway musicians could make surplus distributions to Local 802 so that it might facilitate the process of class transformation through such activities as organizing, educating, surveying, administrating, and negotiating. Inevitably, union by-laws will need to be rewritten to specify how the work is performed, how the orchestra is organized, what the new and/or different responsibilities of the musicians are, and what roles their elected committee representatives have. Local 802 could ensure maximum participation and democracy in the committee election process, and the union may need to redefine the purview of the various committee representatives. For example, the responsibilities of trial board representatives, who are elected to ensure adherence to union guidelines, will need to include methods to retain the Broadway musicians' new communist class process.

Furthermore, the orchestra could make surplus distribution to a personnel representative who they might elect. This new personnel manager might have similar functions as the Designated Contractor who is currently appointed by the MC. After class transformation, this elected representative might implement various structures, methods, and rules to support the new communist class process. Additionally, the orchestras' representatives to the Broadway Theatre Committee will need to support the individual orchestra's communist class process on the Broadway/industry level. These representatives will share events and/or experiences among the various Broadway orchestras. Many of the necessary bureaucratic structures are already in place within Local 802, and the changes just outlined are clearly feasible, provided that the roles and objectives of the various structures are amended.

The musicians will continue to do the same work, receive payments for their work, and toil in the same Broadway theatres.[40] What will change is that the workers themselves will now collectively appropriate and distribute the surplus they produce, thereby making possible workplace improvements. The musicians would make payments to themselves in the form of wages and benefits from the payment received by Local 802 from the Producers. They will also make payments (dues) to Local 802 for the services it provides the Broadway musicians, and these rates might need to be increased from their current level of 3% because of the increase in administrative work that the Union would provide. Conversely, the new system of collective appropriation might be more economical for the Broadway musicians due to a decrease in grievances and their procedural expenses.

If the Broadway musicians desire, after a class transformation they could make surplus distributions to insure that they could have a genuine voice in their work lives, have more of a role in their working environment, and possibly make collective decisions regarding the various problems and issues they encounter. For example, now that the Broadway musicians organize the hiring process, issues of nepotism, favoritism, and discrimination that currently abound in the hiring process could decrease through a self-enforced system of checks and balances. Furthermore, the union could establish a procedure for selecting the orchestra that might include affirmative action requirements to increase the participation of women, Latinos, African-Americans, and younger players. Standards to welcome, train, and hire new Broadway musicians might result in an increase in union membership, since such membership provides access to employment. Furthermore, various alternative work arrangements could be put into practice, such as job sharing programs and provisions for injured, sick, or pregnant musicians. The musicians could design pre-transformation strategies that would facilitate the implementation of such programs, and possibly even initiate them in a current pre-transformative setting.

The musicians can also make significant advances in their pre-transformation work situations by creating a class-transformative agenda. Simply having an agenda may be empowering, and this might in turn motivate the musicians and Local 802 to initiate changes in their present working conditions. Furthermore, musicians' recognition of capitalist surplus extraction by the Producers, that is an awareness of their exploited positions, may make clear to them their relative importance in the production process. Like many other workers, Broadway musicians are not cognizant of their own exploitation. As discussed in Chapter 3, they tend to believe that it is a privilege to be a Broadway musician, and that the employers are displaying their altruism by providing them with this esteemed employment opportunity. Nevertheless, as Thomas Jefferson once counseled, "Enlighten the people generally, and tyranny and oppressions of body and mind will vanish like evil spirits at the dawn of the day" (2). Enlightenment (class-consciousness) may have various consequences, as education typically does, but it is in any case a precondition for change.

Table 4.1 below summarizes some of the desirable outcomes that might be possible after class transformation. As mentioned previously, Local 802, like most other unions, is a service union, providing a commodity (union representation) for a fee (dues), and Local 802 typically ignores the 'pre-transformation' issues. However, after transformation, Local 802 officials' relationship with the musicians will be transformed. Furthermore, in the post-transformative situation envisioned here, the union will continue to provide the services of representation, but under radically different circumstances with regard to the Broadway musicians. The Broadway musicians could make surplus distributions to the union to facilitate and reinforce the communist class process, rather than reinforcing the necessary conditions of existence for capitalist exploitation. Local 802 will continue to negotiate contracts, but the price of the orchestra, not the musicians' wages, will be negotiated. As a result of a series of subtle changes in the union/musician relationship, the union will now take on the role of ensuring the absence of exploitation.[41]

Table 4.1   Pre/Post Transformation Possibilities

Pre-Transformation	Post-Transformation
Exploitation: appropriation of the surplus value by the producer.	Collective appropriation and distribution of the surplus value by the musicians themslves.
Little or no participation over the work environment and hiring process (except for their own substitutes).	More participation over the work environment and hiring process with guidelines established through the union.
Little or no involvement by most Broadway musicians regarding the work process.	Direct participation in the work process by members of the orchestra and/or their elected representatives.
Working on Broadway is quite exclusive and it is difficult for new musicians to enter the field.	More musicians would be willing to join the union because it gives them access to a job in an orchestra.
High degree of favoritism, nepotism, and discrimination in hiring exists.	Nepotism, favoritism, and all forms of gender, racial, and sexual discrimination will be abolished through internal union guidelines.
Grievances are rarely if ever filed because of the fear of not being chosen for the next show. Rabble-rousing is punished.	Grievances and problems would be addressed internally.
No provisions for alternative work arrangements, such as job sharing.	As a collective the orchestra could make decisions about alternative work arrangements and tasks.

The union, then, can improve the status of its members by facilitating a class-transformative agenda. Furthermore, simply by having such an agenda, the union can introduce workplace improvements before the transformation: often, collective strength develops simply from having a plan that addresses a specific issue. Finally, a class-transformative agenda might prove to be appropriate for other unions as well, and it might succeed in reversing the social status decline of trade unionism.

The social perspective of trade unions is often quite negative: even union members, including Local 802 musicians, view 'big labor' as monopolistic, greedy, stubborn, and undemocratic (Freeman and Medoff). By shifting the union's mission to include class transformation and focusing on participatory democracy, the musicians' perception of Local 802 might improve. After transformation, it will be imperative for the musicians to increase their participation in union affairs and workplaces, and this should have an empowering and liberating effect on the members. Additionally, Local 802's position with its members will be altered in that it will be accountable for communist subsumed-class payments it receives. This change might result in member empowerment, fewer allegations of corruption, fewer behind the scenes 'off the record' meetings, and other issues of concern to the members.

In a class transformative system, the musicians and Local 802 would make decisions about their organization. That is, they would manage and regulate surplus distributions for issues like orchestra personnel hiring, workers' salaries, fringe benefit allocations, and related administrative and personnel costs.[42] The social relationship between Local 802 and the Broadway musicians is but one relationship that will change post-transformation. The relationship the union and the Broadway musicians have with their various constituencies will also be altered.

2. The Capitalist Producers

Broadway Producers' positions as capitalists, in most respects, will not change post class transformation. Whatever legal formation the Producers choose, should it be a partnership, limited liability company, or corporation, will have no compromising effect on the musicians' class transformation or their relationship with other Broadway agents. Rather than buying the commodity labor power from the musicians individually, as they do currently, in a post-transformation arrangement the Producers simply buy the intact communist commodity, music, from Local 802 and make direct payments to the union for the subsequent distribution to the musicians.

At present, the Producers distribute the surplus value to those who provide their conditions of existence as capitalists; these payments to most of the Producers' constituencies would more than likely continue post-transformation. Indeed, notwithstanding the Producers' altered post-transformation relationship with the musicians, the capitalist Producer might remain a capitalist with regard to other social relations. That is, the capitalist Producers will continue to make necessary payments to individuals, firms, and the State to ensure their own continued existence and reproduction as capitalists. The recipients of surplus value distributions hold a subsumed class position and provide services and products necessary for a Broadway Musical. For example, the city of New York holds a subsumed class position because surplus value payments are made to it in the form of taxes, payment of which provides the Producers with services such as police protection, fire protection, traffic control and even advertising.

The government, however, is but one subsumed class occupant. Others include investors, directors, choreographers, stage mangers, dance coaches, stagehands, ushers, ticket takers, cleaning personnel, etc. More than likely, most, if not all, of these payments to these subsumed class occupants will be unchanged post class transformation. Furthermore, many of the fundamental class positions held by other workers, such as the actors, would remain unchanged, unless of course any of these agents initiate their own transformation(s). For example, should the Broadway actors decide that the new class positions held by the musicians are preferable to their present situation; they may indeed advocate for similar reforms through their union, Actors' Equity.

The Producers, now merchant capitalists vis-à-vis their new relationship with the musicians, will buy the commodity 'music for a Broadway production.' The Producers will then resell the commodity music during the show with the intent on profiting from the sale of the music during the Broadway production. Just as if the Producers were to buy recorded music, the commodity 'music' would now be considered part of the means of production and the Producers would make non-class exchange payments for this commodity. Thus, the capitalist Producer would remain a productive capitalist with respect to the production of the musical; however, the relationship with the musicians is transformed, if ever so subtly.

3. Music Coordinators

One of the desired results of class transformation is that the choices the Broadway musicians make regarding new communist surplus distributions will improve the musicians' working situation. For example, if the Broadway musicians decide to retain the services of a MC to form orchestras, as is currently the practice, the musicians themselves would be the MC's employers. Under the current system, the Producers make a capitalist subsumed-class payment to the MCs for this service, but under the new system, this position would no longer exist. If the musicians retain the MC's services post-transformation, then it would be the musicians who would employ the MC. The musicians themselves will make the payments for the MC's services; i.e., a communist subsumed class payment and the musicians themselves would only make this payment if they believed and collectively agreed that such a payment secures their conditions of existence in a communist class structure. Conversely, the musicians might opt to discontinue the services of the MCs entirely because such services might now be considered redundant.

As previously discussed, the five Broadway MCs have almost absolute control over the Broadway musicians, especially with regard to the hiring process, and if a musician somehow falls out of favor with the MC, his/her chances of working on Broadway again are minimal at best. Post class transformation, the MC's services will be superfluous because the musicians under the guidance of Local 802 could themselves provide an orchestra through whatever method they deem appropriate. For example, as will be discussed in Chapter 5, the Broadway musicians might use a hiring hall situation as they did in the past. Or, they could adopt a more democratic arrangement in which Local 802 and its agents could facilitate the auditions that were proposed above.

Historically, the MC was required to be both a union member and a member of the orchestra for the Broadway musical for which s/he was hired, holding the title of "designated contractor" in the collective bargaining agreement. Over time this relationship has been much modified. There still exists a "designated" or "in-house" contractor, but his/her role is relegated to one of personnel manager; all that remains is the requirement that the designated/in-house contractor be a playing musician.[43] Currently, and though contractually obligated, Local 802 has no input into the selection of either the designated/in-house contractor or the MC. There is no review by the Executive Board, nor are the musicians engaged through designated/in-house contractors. A class transformation strategy might be to reemploy this dormant provision, abating or possibly eliminating the power wielded by the MCs. The Producers undoubtedly will resist, citing current practices as a viable precedent; however, eliminating or even the threat of eliminating the MC's position could provoke an immediate change in management techniques and attitudes. Currently, the MC is the leading threat to a musician's job security, and job security is one of the musician's most salient issues.[44] The strategy just described might improve musicians' working conditions prior to class transformation because of the collective challenge to the power of the MCs. When challenged, the MCs might make adjustments to their absolute authority in the hiring process.

4. Theatre Owners

Both pre and post-transformation the theatre owner holds a capitalist subsumed class position vis-à-vis the Producer. As landlord, in return for providing access to a Broadway theatre, s/he receives a subsumed class payment in the form of rent. A subtle change will probably be required with regard to the Broadway musicians though. As discussed in Chapter 2, the theatre owner is the employer of record for all Broadway musicians except the conductor.[45] In the prototype discussed above, there should be no modification in the theatre owner's position as landlord; however, his/her role as the musicians' employer of record would cease to exist. Recall from Chapters 2 and 3, that although the theatre owners are the employer of record, they have no role in hiring, firing, and supervising the Broadway musicians. The theatre owners' of record position vis-à-vis the musicians is one that is antiquated and only remains because of tradition.[46] In the post-transformative arrangement, the theatre owners would have no legal connection with the musicians, unless of course they are the Producers of the show in question. Nonetheless, this would be a minor adjustment to the current situation in that the theatre owner is only anachronistically the musicians' employer in any case.

5. The League

The Broadway League currently holds the subsumed class position vis-à-vis the capitalist Producers as a labor relations specialist and contract negotiator. For these services, the Producers (and theatre owners) make subsumed class payments in the form of dues to the League. In a post-transformation domain, the relationship between the Producers and the League would not necessarily change; however, contract talks and grievances between the musicians and the Producers might be noticeably different. The Producers' representative, the League, will now negotiate over the price of an orchestra, not wages or benefits. The cost of the wages and benefits would be part of the price of the orchestra as now restructured. Negotiations over working conditions, however, might receive similar attention in that it is the Producers and the theatre owners who provide such conditions.

6. The Conductors

In a post-transformation environment, the conductors may experience significant changes. As previously illustrated, conductors qua orchestra leaders are surplus producing (productive) workers. As such, in a communist class process, they, like the side-musicians,[47] will collectively produce and distribute the surplus. In a pre-transformation setting, the Producer directly hires the conductor and is his/her employer of record, but post-transformation this occupational relationship will in all probability no longer be viable. The musicians themselves will, hopefully, develop a democratic selection/election process for the conductor.[48] The process by which the musicians select their orchestra leaders is of minor concern here; the important aspect is the conductors' role in surplus appropriation and distribution. If the conductors are part of the collective in the communist class process of music production, then they must retain a position as appropriator and distributor of the surplus.

Conversely, should the conductors choose not to, or somehow they are restricted from, participating in the Broadway musicians' collective and they retain their current employment situation as a capitalist worker vis-à-vis the Producer, a capitalist class relationship between the conductor and Producer would simultaneously exist with the Broadway musicians that are producing a communist commodity. Although the Producer could continue to hire and pay wages to the conductor to lead the orchestra, in this type of arrangement, the conductor's position as an exploited capitalist worker (surplus value producer and not appropriator) will remain. In this example, the side-musicians of the orchestra would be collectively appropriating/distributing their own surplus while being led by a capitalist fundamental class worker. With such an arrangement, both a capitalist (conductor) and communist (side musicians) fundamental class process will exist in the orchestra pit concurrently.

Moreover, the portion of the surplus produced by the conductor will continue to be appropriated and subsequently distributed by the Producer, which in itself might instigate a conflict with the musicians over size of the surplus portion produced by the conductor. It is also possible that because of his/her role as agent for the Producer, the conductor would no longer be invited to participate in the communist measures set by the musicians. Moreover, as an agent of the Producer, the conductors' allegiance to the union and the side-musicians might be compromised and other conflicts between the conductors and musicians could ensue, including conflicts over the extent of supervisory duties granted to the conductor, about which side-musicians are chosen as orchestra members, or more likely, regarding the particular size of an orchestra due to the Producer's resistance to minimum requirements.

Conflicts between the conductors qua orchestra leader and the side-musicians might be further exacerbated by the simultaneous position many Broadway conductors hold as Music Director (MD). As discussed in Chapter 2, many Broadway conductors hold the non-bargaining unit position as Music Director and thereby have more responsibilities in the production of a Broadway musical than merely leading the orchestra. They may write transition scores or be part of the initial 'creative team'; moreover, they have complete control over anything that has to do with the show's music. In their current positions, MDs receive a capitalist subsumed class payment for this service from the Producers. Hence, in a pre-transformation setting, the conductor qua MD holds two class positions, a surplus value producer as conductor and a subsumed class recipient of surplus value.

Should the conductor be hired as the MD in a post-transformation setting; it is possible that s/he could be part of the communist collective in his/her role as conductor while simultaneously holding a subsumed class position as MD. Additionally, if the conductor's position remains within the capitalist realm, s/he would be in a similar position as s/he is pre-transformation: a capitalist surplus value producer as conductor and a surplus value recipient as MD. The important point here is to ensure that the musicians (including the conductor if possible) secure their conditions of existence as a communist collective. Therefore, it is imperative that the class and non-class positions are explicitly defined. This will hopefully circumvent challenges to the new communist class process developed by the Broadway musicians.

F. CONCLUSION

From the analysis provided above, one can envision many other possible outcomes or changes that the Broadway musicians could employ or might encounter. What has been provided here is simply a basic schematic to demonstrate how class transformation is not only an abstract theoretical exercise, but also, and possibly more importantly, a concrete example of how class transformation is possible for the Broadway musicians' workplace. With Local 802's facilitation, the Broadway musicians indeed could employ revolutionary tactics that would transform them from exploited capitalist workers into workers in a communist collective which would, under particular circumstances, improve their working conditions.

Many of the present concerns of the Broadway musicians might be negated via class transformation. However, the mere exercising of class transformative agendas and strategies by Local 802 and the Broadway musicians could indeed have positive affects on the musicians' current work situation. In the next, concluding chapter, the possibility of a class-transformative arrangement given prior union experiences will be explored. Furthermore, the concerns of the Broadway musicians discussed in Chapter 3 will be revisited in a post-transformation setting, or a setting with simply a class transformative agenda. Finally, there will be a brief discussion on how other workers' organizations, whether union or not, might take the information provided in this book and apply it to their own situations.

5 Post Class Transformation
Applications on Broadway and Beyond

A. INTRODUCTION

The previous chapters studied the potential of class transformation for the Broadway musicians and the reasons why they should employ a class-transformative strategy. Each chapter in this book focused on the critical role unions should play in the class transformation process. That is, unions should be both facilitating and implementing class transformation. In the prototype proposed in Chapter 4, the Broadway musicians form their own orchestras and then sell the services of the full orchestra to a Producer. This relatively subtle change enables the Broadway musicians to eradicate their current exploitative situation—from capitalist exploited workers to communist non-exploited workers. In order to fully explain how and why the Broadway musicians will be better off post-transformation than without one, issues examined in Chapter 3 such as safety and health, worker participation, and job security will be further analyzed. This class transformation is revolutionary, but it is not a utopian dream. In this chapter I provide concrete examples of how this transformation can be accomplished.

The Broadway musicians have enjoyed many successes throughout the years with the help of their union, including real wage increases and lucrative benefits. In this sense, the union has resisted "the encroachments of capital" (Marx, *Value* 62); however, hitherto Local 802 has not made any efforts to change the class structure under which the Broadway musicians toil—a failure of trade unions according to Marx. That is, the Broadway musicians are not "emancipated" from capitalist exploitation. In the proposed prototype Local 802 will continue to provide services such as negotiating contracts and grievance representation; however, under the revised structure, with surplus distributions made by the Broadway musicians, Local 802 will take on additional tasks such as auditioning, hiring, and organizing the musicians into an orchestra. There may be a need for more participation from the Broadway musicians, more administrative duties for the union and its members, an increased level of organization and changes to Local 802's by-laws, to complete the tasks that were traditionally assumed by management. That is, there will be bona fide self-governance of surplus distributions, therefore the Broadway musicians and Local 802 will assume many 'managerial' tasks. While self-governance and class transformation might be burdensome, particularly during the early stages of implementation, the rewards of transformation might include emancipation from exploitation that manifests into better health and safety regulations, more worker participation and job security. The benefits that should outweigh the inconveniences.

This concluding chapter commences with a discussion of the possibility for change and how the building trades' unions offer a potential model for the musicians. This is followed by an historical perspective of how the musicians, at one time, used a hiring hall at the Roseland Ballroom that could be used as a basic template for the Broadway musicians—although with modernization—in a post class-transformative setting. Both of these models are provided to demonstrate how Local 802 and even the musicians themselves have or have had the internal union structural framework to facilitate and process a revolution. The models are also provided for an understanding of how the trades' unions currently, and the musician's union in the past, did not take the next 'revolutionary' step of eradicating exploitation because of their class-blindness, even though both had a significant voice in the hiring process. These models provide a template or at least a starting place for interested in class transformation.

Subsequent to the discussion of the two models of the building trades' unions and the Roseland Hiring hall, I provide an illustration of how the Broadway musicians might negate any or all of the concerns addressed in Chapter 3 within a new setting. As was discussed in Chapter 3, the Broadway musicians encounter many of the same issues that workers in other industries face. While the musicians have resisted the intrusions by their capitalist employer with some success, the musicians' class-blindness has prevented a reversal of the many problems they face and, worse yet, engendered an acceptance of the status quo particularly in the hiring process. NMCA creates an avenue from which the unions and their members can reevaluate their current situation and make the necessary improvements.

The conclusion offers other union researchers suggestions on why and how a class-transformative strategy using NMCA in their particular situation might be beneficial; thus giving these workers and their advocates the opportunity to transform their own exploitative situation and improve their own working conditions. The basic premise has been to demonstrate how unions can play a critical role in changing the class structure of their members and that this is absolutely possible—not utopian as some radical commentators may suggest. Unions can achieve such results by rejecting class-blind strategies and employ NMCA; the result might be a cumulative political rejection of the conservative social agenda besides workplace improvements.

B. THE POSSIBILITY FOR CHANGE

1. The Building Trades' Model

Samuel Gompers' pronouncement that any change in the economic structure is a "pie in the sky" belief is erroneous. Gompers' however, was not alone in this line of thought; even many so-called radical thinkers believe that any transformation from capitalism to communism is a utopian futuristic ideal that cannot be attained any time soon. On the contrary though, as was shown in the previous chapter, when analyzing a site of production using NMCA, the possibility of change is much more attainable. Furthermore, with subtle changes in their own work environments and structure, other unions could facilitate their own transformation. Unions do not have to make drastic changes with their procedures or structure to make class transformation possible. The building trades' unions present a model in which only subtle changes would be necessary for class transformation.

An arrangement (prototype) such as the one described in the prior chapter is not without a similar precedent, although arguably not communist.[1] Prime examples are the many building trades' unions such as the plumbers, carpenters, laborers, and electricians. The building trades' model illustrates a primary stage of implementing the prototype the Broadway musicians might take towards the goal of a communist class structure. Trades' unions have roles unlike the responsibilities of industrial unions. Industrial unions typically represent every worker in a particular workplace no matter what level of skill or position. An example of an industrial union is the United Auto Workers (UAW). In a union factory, the UAW represents every non-supervisory worker in that particular plant. Conversely, trades unions represent a group of workers who share a particular craft, such as carpentry or cabinet making.

Becoming a member of a trades union is often a difficult process. A potential member must take rigorous written and skill exams and have experience in the particular trade for which s/he is applying. Moreover, accusations of nepotistic treatment of potential members have plagued trades' unions for some time now. Often, the best paying construction jobs are union jobs; therefore both union and non-union workers covet these positions. If a particular construction job uses a union contractor, then the workers must be union members. So not only does the union restrict access to membership, they subsequently restrict access to the jobs.[2]

Once accepted into the union, new members (apprentices) are required to undergo rigorous training, both on-the-job[3] and in the classroom, and each new member must enroll in a college program that is specific to that particular craft. The probationary/apprenticeship training process may take as much as five years if uninterrupted. For example, in Indiana the Plumbers and Steamfitters administer a joint apprenticeship program with employing contractors. In order to get his/her journeyman's card, an apprentice must finish a 5 year program that includes classroom skills and on the job training as well as traditional college courses that include English, history, and mathematics. Upon successful completion of the apprenticeship program, the graduate receives an associate's degree in 'Construction Technology.' The trades' unions play a significant role in the education process including hiring instructors and providing the training facility. In Fort Wayne, Indiana for example, Local 166 of the Plumbers and Steamfitters has an extensive training facility with 6 classrooms. Thus, the Plumbers and Steamfitters not only restrict employment—they believe they also ensure quality production.

Each building trades' union has a local 'hiring hall' in which union members congregate or wait to be called for specific employment in their fields under a union contract. Each union has their own process regarding the hiring process, but what is important to this discussion is that it is the unions which decide who goes to work and who does not. For example, most of the building trades require that a member must be in 'good standing' in order to be called into work. Good standing might mean a variety of things to particular unions. However, in every union a member can only be in good standing if s/he is current with his/her dues.

Building trades' union members are put to work when a contractor calls the hiring hall and requests that the union sends the needed workers to a specified job site. Typically, the union member will go to work with his/her own tools and be prepared to do even the most complicated tasks. Building trades' unions pride themselves on the fact that the union workers are highly skilled and trained, thus giving contractors the incentive of hiring union workers.

When the union building tradespersons show up at the job site, any similarity to the communist class arrangement proposed in the previous chapter ends. The workers simply get to the site, the contractor then hires them and pays them the hourly wage dictated in the respective trades' collective bargaining agreement. Building trades' workers, once hired by the contractor are then subject to exploitation just as in any other capitalist class relationship. Like the Broadway musicians, building trades workers may or may not supply their own tools and transportation. However important owning ones tools are, that fact alone is not the defining aspect of capitalism; production, appropriation, and distribution of the surplus value defines the class structure. That is, tradespersons produce surplus value for the capitalist, for which they are not paid.

Building trades' unions could also facilitate a communist class process for their own members through a similar to the arrangement outlined in the previous chapter. The building trades' unions have many of the institutions and structures already in place that would make forming a communist collective a very attainable possibility. These union members could also organize themselves into a collective where they both produce and appropriate the surplus embodied in the newly produced commodity, in this case a new house for example.

With surplus distributions from the Broadway musicians, Local 802 may do as the building trades have done and arrange a hiring hall and train their members. Additionally the Broadway musicians could also adopt such a training and certification program like the building trades' unions. A program such as this would ensure a level of quality that might not only facilitate the hiring process for the Broadway musicians, but also ensure that the best possible orchestra was 'sold' to the Producers. Local 802's headquarters on 48th Street in New York City has ample space in which to achieve these goals. Additionally, there are many skilled and talented retired musicians who might even volunteer for instructional services. Moreover, the musicians did at one time have a hiring hall similar to the trades' union model, so the infrastructure for these changes is in the common memory of many musicians.

2. A Historical Perspective: Roseland Hiring Hall

In the mid-20th century, Local 802 ran a hiring hall for its members at the Roseland Ballroom, in the heart of midtown Manhattan's theatre district on West 52nd Street. From 1952 through 1982, Local 802's headquarters were located on the second floor of the same building which houses the infamous Roseland Ballroom in what is now the Virginia Theatre. Every Monday, Wednesday[4] and Friday afternoon, contractors for club-date offices and bandleaders would come to the 'floor,' as the hiring hall was known, to find musicians to perform in the following weekend's events.[5] The hiring process on the floor did not have a bona fide structure. Musicians gathered there and the contractors and bandleaders came in and chose the musicians they preferred. According to Leo Ball, a long-time Local 802 member, "many thousands of musicians" would be present during the hiring process. He described the process as:

> . . . intimidating a situation as could be imagined. On the stage sat a single man with a table and a microphone, and directly in front of him, musicians and contractors ten deep, screaming up names to be paged. At the same time, to the left of the stage, was another person with a mike, sitting in front of a bank of about 20 telephones, calling names of musicians receiving outside calls, usually from contractors not able to come to the floor, or other musicians asking friends to see if they might pick up the weekend for them' (*E-mail*).

Their preferences were based on reputation or "through contacts on a personal basis" (Press, *E-mail*). Orchestras, however, were not 'sold' as a unit because the 'floor' was not open to "outside employers" (Ball, *E-mail*).[6] Thus, the contractors and leaders chose individual musicians and formed orchestras to meet the needs of the specific event. The contractors and leaders signed the standard Local 802 club-date contracts[7] and paid the musicians themselves. "As the work in club dates became more and more dominated by a few offices and the work itself started to diminish, the need for the 'floor' became less important" (Ball, *E-Mail*). By the 1990s, the 'floor' ceased to exist (Ball, *Wednesdays*).

The 'floor' was not only important for musicians' employment, but also to socialize. Often groups of musicians would meet for a meal or drinks after the floor closed. It was camaraderie that many musicians remember fondly. The 'floor' was also a place where musicians made vital contacts with contractors, leaders, and other musicians, making such connections is how musicians typically gained access to work. Even though the musicians were in direct competition with each other for the available engagements, the 'floor' also provided a sense of community and solidarity amongst the musicians, of which there is currently no equivalent. The Roseland hiring hall was not a workers' collective of surplus appropriators and distributors. Nonetheless, what history does imply is that one of the primary stages of a communist class process, the hiring phase, and the tenor of solidarity and community has previously existed. To achieve this again, Local 802 could establish a new hiring hall arrangement. Alternatively, Local 802 could utilize technological advances like email, computer databases, and cell phones to establish a 'virtual' hiring hall that requires very little physical space. On the other hand, Local 802 could incorporate such a hall into its current residence on 48th street in midtown Manhattan. Whatever the arrangement, the union can provide a space, virtual or otherwise, for the musicians to come together periodically to receive and distribute the surplus, thus facilitating the communist class process.

A surplus distribution by the Broadway musicians could be made to develop a database of Broadway musicians that categorizes musicians by instrument, genre, and experience. The Broadway musicians' committee could use such a database to arrange orchestras to the Producers' specifications. Conversely, the musicians could hire a manager to perform this task and would make a surplus distribution payment to the database manager for this service.[8] The Broadway musicians' committee could set forth guidelines for the manager and the hiring process. These guidelines could include democratic hiring standards, such as a seniority clause, a revolving list, or whatever system the musicians prefer.[9] The chosen musicians could then meet at the union hall and mutually elect a conductor from a 'conductors' database. Conversely, the conductor might be secured prior to the side-musicians so that s/he might participate in orchestra's selection, much like the current practice on Broadway.[10] Or, the musicians could give the manager the authority to select a conductor.[11] Whatever the process, there is no challenge to the communist class process as long as the musicians, including the conductor, appropriate the surplus labor they produce. Indeed, should the Broadway musicians and the conductors, who are the surplus labor producers, choose to hire managers to organize an orchestra or even administer the surplus distributions, there is no challenge to the communist class process as long as the managers remain subordinate to them (Resnick and Wolff, *Class Theory* 19). Although this simple transformation by the Broadway musicians is revolutionary, it does not require any change to the basic capitalist structure of musical production nor does it have to alter the actual job of the musicians.

The two models, the trades' unions and the Roseland Hiring hall, allow one to envision a structure that Broadway musicians or any other group of workers' may employ to eradicate their own exploitative situations. As these models show, unions have had or now have various structures in place. Moreover, unionists can use these internal structures as a starting place for class change. Additionally, the models reject the notion that the workers cannot themselves engage in processes traditionally controlled by capitalists, particularly the hiring process. Unionists can take these models and extend them just a bit farther to include a class-transformative agenda.

Because the building trades and the Broadway musicians share the same craft with their co-workers, using the prototype provided here might not be practical or attainable in an industrial setting. Nonetheless, what can be extended to other types of unions is the use of class as an analytical tool. As Marx inferred, class-blindness is a reason for the failures of trade union movement. If analysts employed class as their entry point for investigation, the existence of various forms of exploitation would be exposed and what might follow is an improvement in working conditions. The next section contains a discussion of how the Broadway musicians' working conditions might be improved because of this class analysis.

C. SUBJECTS OF CONCERN FOR THE BROADWAY MUSICIANS REVISITED

Chapter 3 incorporated a variety of hazards Broadway musicians currently endure; with the simple class transformation proposed here, some if not all of these concerns might be rectified given the musicians' new class structure. As mentioned, the issues about which the musicians had the greatest concern were safety and health, worker participation, and job security. The discussion that follows is hypothetical, but it will show the possibility of improvement given a class transformation. Hypothetical or not, the discussion should incite readers to think of possible strategies for reorganizing their own work arrangements.

1. Safety and Health

Recall that the primary safety and health issues discussed in Chapter 3 were concerns over the increased use of special effects and elaborate scenery, the increased reliance by Producers on amplified music, and repetitive stress disorders. While some of these concerns might not be totally eliminated in a post class transformation, open and candid conversations without fear of job loss or the decreased prospect of future positions might be achieved. Currently, when musicians raise concerns about any detrimental health conditions occurring during their work, the MC takes note and may indeed retaliate against the musician in the future. In a post-transformative setting, the musicians could discuss any concerns amongst themselves and make collective decisions on how best to address the situation. They might make surplus distributions to eliminate any hazardous conditions. Although some would claim that this practice is similar to what Broadway musicians currently employ, that is, the musicians now often discuss any potential hazards within their orchestras, some musicians remain silent because of the threat of reprisal. Typically the musicians alert Local 802 representatives of any potential hazards through confidential or anonymous telephone calls. The union representative then visits the orchestra pit in question and 'discovers' the hazard for herself.[12] Subsequently Local 802 files grievances on the musicians' behalf without mention of any particular musician's involvement or notification. Post-transformation this might not be the case because of the collective decision-making and open conversations Local 802 might encourage or possibly even require, so that the musicians can resolve such issues among themselves. The musicians might include these discussions during their periodic surplus distribution meetings.

In a post-transformation setting, the musicians might employ 'job sharing' to provide relief from health concerns including inhaling caustic gases, fumes and particulates, being subject to extremely loud amplified music, and experiencing repetitive stress injuries. For example, two musicians might share the same position. In the pre-transformation setting, one Broadway musician occupies one 'chair' or position. If the musician chooses to absent him/herself at anytime, it is the responsibility of the chair-holding musician to find him/herself a substitute. The Broadway musicians venerate the current substitution process; nonetheless, in a post-transformation setting the process might be more equitable. In the current situation, the musicians often choose their friends or other musicians who in the past have chosen them to substitute, i.e., a quid pro quo arrangement for which the musician might be unintentionally guilty of discrimination or nepotism. In the post-transformation setting, a shared position would decrease the exposure to any harmful health effects if so chosen. Local 802 and the musicians could develop a process that might encourage affirmative action and other preferable hiring arrangements. Furthermore, they might even make surplus distributions to those musicians who perform under hazardous conditions, thus supplementing his/her wage if s/he worked fewer hours than full-time.

A shared position might also provide access to Broadway jobs to some musicians who might not have been able to take a chair in the past. For example, if for some reason one musician could only work days and another musician could only work nights, then these two musicians could share the position. Typically there are only three daytime matinees on Broadway; therefore, in this situation, the daytime musician would work only three shows per week, meanwhile the evening musician would work five shows. Depending on how the Broadway musicians make provisions for substitutions, each musician holding a shared position would therefore be responsible for his/her own schedule. If this arrangement is something desired by the musicians, again, they could make surplus distributions to supplement the workers sharing a position.

As for the substitution process, the Broadway musicians and Local 802 might make surplus distributions to develop a substitution system that is more democratic than the one currently in place. The musicians could organize a database that includes information regarding musicians' skills and instruments. If a substitute were needed, the database would be employed to find a musician for the particular time in question. Again, Local 802 could facilitate this process by creating and maintaining the database paid for by the musicians with distributions from the surplus. Additionally, Local 802 could monitor the substitution process so that there was an equitable distribution of the work. Thus, a job-sharing program would not only alleviate some of the health consequences faced by musicians during their work, it might also allow for a more democratic assignment of duties. If a more democratic process is a principal issue for the Broadway musicians, then surplus distributions might be necessary for their implementation. Surplus distributions might also be made to a Local 802 staff representative for monitoring the substitution process and organizing the job-sharing program. Additionally, a surplus distribution might be made to the musicians who share a position if this is something that the musicians believe is consistent with their ideology or simply because they think it is an endeavor worth pursuing.

2. Worker Participation

It may seem obvious to many that within a communist structure, one that is truly collective, the workers would have much more say in their work environments than they do in an exploitative capitalist structure, but this does not necessarily need to be the case. Democratic work environments may be more possible within a communist class structure via particular surplus distributions, therefore, Local 802 might assume a role in ensuring that each worker has a 'voice' and participates in a democratic fashion under the communist arrangement proposed above. That is, it would be the union's as well as its members' responsibility to make sure workers' voices were not stifled. Again, the Broadway musicians and Local 802 could set standards and change by-laws that represent their own proclivity for democracy. Distributions from the surplus might be made to a union representative to organize such a democratic structure.

In a post-transformative setting the Broadway musicians could collectively make decisions on many aspects of their work, including who gets hired for a particular position. The musicians could assemble their own orchestras and decide on various positions and salaries, which might depend on criteria such as seniority, something completely absent in the pre-transformation setting. Moreover, the Broadway musicians would be able to discuss amongst themselves any issues or problems associated with a particular musician. That is, the musicians would self-monitor and therefore self-discipline any rogue musician. The musicians themselves could decide on penalties assigned to other musicians who stray from the rules. Of course, surplus distributions might be made to the 'enforcers' for their time. Conversely, the musicians could celebrate and reward musicians for various services or good deeds performed by a particular musician. For example, if a Broadway musician volunteered at an underprivileged public school, this action might gain respect and possibly a monetary award presented to the particular musician by his/her fellow Broadway musicians. That is, a surplus distribution would be made to this benevolent musician. The important point, however, is that it would be up to the musicians themselves to collectively determine penalties and rewards for individuals' actions. Worker voice and collective decision-making could secure communist conditions of existence for the Broadway musicians.

To further secure communist conditions of existence, the Broadway musicians could also be jointly responsible for deciding how many orchestra members a particular production will need. This decision could be one done by the musicians' representative with the orchestrator, the music director, and the conductor. There are also creative limitations regarding orchestrations that the Broadway musicians would have to consider when making such decisions. The musicians would negotiate a fee for the services of the orchestra with the Producer and then make their own decision on how many or how few musicians are employed.[13]

The Broadway musicians might also negotiate or insist on being part of the 'creative team' if that is what they wish to do. The musicians could elect, appoint, or assign a representative to a Production's creative team whose primary interest would be to ensure that the musicians' best interests were taken into account. This creative team representative might receive a surplus distribution for his/her additional responsibility for this service. For example, the representative could make it known that extreme sound amplification would not be necessary if more musicians were used. At the very least, the representative could make the other creative team members understand some of the issues the musicians encounter while performing. Currently, no orchestra member is part of the creative team, thus any potential problems are not circumvented prior to the commencement of a musical. In a communist class arrangement like the prototype developed in Chapter 4, worker participation in the pre-production process might be reinforced by the musicians' inclusion on the creative team.

3. Job Security

Of all the concerns that the Broadway musicians face, job security is the most pressing. Currently, the Broadway musicians' job security lasts only for the duration of the production in which they have a chair (position). Musicians can be fired only for "just cause," (League, *Collective Bargaining Agreement* 16) which is a rare occasion on Broadway because it is cumbersome and sometimes difficult for the employer to establish such a case against the musician in question. Substitutes, on the other hand, have no job security because the 'just cause' provision in the collective bargaining agreement does not apply to them, so they can be hired and fired at any time. As stated in the previous two chapters, though the musician holding the position in a Broadway orchestra may enjoy some level of job security for the particular production s/he is currently employed, the security is temporary and no guarantee of future employment exists.

In a pre-transformation setting, the primary obstruction to the Broadway musicians' job security is the capricious and arbitrary decisions made by the MCs, those individuals who hire and fire musicians for Broadway productions. In a post-transformative setting, the role of the MC becomes redundant and the MC's responsibilities might be transferred to the Broadway musicians and Local 802. The Broadway musicians and Local 802 will need to develop policies and procedures for hiring, rehiring, rewarding and disciplining members. These policies and processes can be approved by a full vote of all Broadway musicians or through elected or appointed representatives. If the latter is chosen, then those representatives would be directly obliged to the musicians. Surplus distributions could be made to the elected or appointed representatives for their services or volunteers could be elected volunteers. Either way it will be the Broadway musicians' decision regarding these former managerial tasks.

Although bureaucratic, administrative, legal, or general resistance to change might impede the progress of class transformation, simply having a class-transformative agenda might address some of the issues Broadway musicians encounter, particularly job security. If for example, the MCs believed their positions were being threatened or even questioned in a structured manner by Local 802 and the musicians, they might decide to alter their behavior to the advantage of the musicians. Furthermore, Local 802 currently has disciplinary procedures through a 'trial board,' which could be utilized to penalize MCs' anti-union behavior. This possibility has never been used against a Broadway MC, and the threat of its use might provoke better behavior by the MCs. Ultimately, however, the goal of class transformation is to eradicate exploitation; this would require more than just a change in MCs' behavior. It would require the collective production and appropriation of surplus.

D. CONCLUSION

Unions have a role in eradicating capitalist exploitation, which is not the utopian futuristic enormity that critics contend. Eradicating exploitation is quite possible under the economic structure facing workers today. Unions, particularly Local 802, have been successful in many ways at resisting capitalist encroachment; however, now with the assistance of NMCA, there is the potential for even more successes. Union density and therefore the subsequent decrease in the effectiveness of unions have been in decline for the last 25 years. While union officials from the AFL-CIO to individual local unions have made many attempts to counter this decline, most have been unsuccessful. It is time for radical change, including changes in how workers are perceived and how work is arranged. As this book has shown, radical changes including class-transformation are indeed possible with the assistance of unions and the implementation of NMCA strategies.

In the NMCA context, communism is indeed possible and unions have the responsibility to develop various techniques for its implementation. The prototype presented in this book includes only modest changes in work organization for the Broadway musicians; however the results are radical and may have far-reaching effects. While it is recognized that workers in different industries have unique circumstances, what they have in common with the Broadway musicians is capitalist exploitation. Therefore, other unions and worker organizations can use this book and NMCA as a model for changes in their own situation. The first step, however, is to eliminate the class-blindness of unions and their advocates via NMCA, which subsequently will guide workers to eliminate capitalist exploitation.

Through NMCA, the Broadway musicians have the opportunity to make significant improvements in their work and possible their private lives by implementing communism into their workplace. With capitalist exploitation eliminated, the musicians may no longer believe their jobs are in jeopardy because of the capricious and arbitrary actions of the MCs. Furthermore, the redundancy of the MC position and, therefore, its subsequent elimination may lead to a less stressful work environment, which may result in a more peaceful private life. Additionally, in a communist arrangement, the Broadway musicians could make considerable improvements in most if not all aspects of their working lives by making complementary surplus distributions. Such changes and improvements become visible once the Broadway musicians' class-blindness is renounced; a NMCA has the capacity to meet these ends. Unions, including Local 802 must be responsible to their members and therefore should make strenuous attempts to demonstrate capitalist exploitation and its effects on workers' lives and livelihoods. This book demonstrated the possibility of a communist workplace and exploitation eradication for the Broadway musicians. If implemented the musicians will reap the rewards.

APPENDIX A

MEMORANDUM OF AGREEMENT BETWEEN THE LEAGUE OF AMERICAN THEATRES & PRODUCERS B.V. THEATRICAL VENTURES, INC. MUSICAL RIGHTS INC. AND ASSOCIATED MUSICIANS OF GREATER NEW YORK, LOCAL 802, AFM, AFL-CIO

This Agreement between The League of American Theatres & Producers, B.V. Theatrical Ventures, Inc. ("BVTVI"), Musical Rights Inc. ("MRI") (collectively the "employers") and Associated Musicians of Greater New York, Local 802, AFM, AFL-CIO, extends the parties expired collective bargaining agreements until March 5, 2007 to the extent such agreements are not modified by, or inconsistent with, the terms and conditions set forth herein. All other provisions of the expired agreements remain unchanged.

1. Article III Wages Scales

a. Minimum weekly wages shall be increased as follows:
Effective and retroactive to 3/11/03: $20
9/1/03: $15
3/1/04: $20
9/6/04: $15
3/7/05: $20
9/5/05: $20
3/6/06: $20
9/9/06: $20

b. In addition, the wage rates set forth in Article IV, Sections B, C, 2A(1), (2) and (3), and Section D, plus those contained in Schedules A and B (orchestrators and arrangers), shall be increased by the following percentages on the following dates:

Effective Date	% Increase
3/11/03	1.54%
9/1/03	1.14%
3/1/04	1.50%
9/6/04	1.11%
3/7/05	1.46%
9/5/05	1.44%
3/6/06	1.42%
9/9/06	1.40%

c. Section A (1) (a—d) are deleted.

d. Section C shall be modified to provide that: "the Employer/Producer and Conductor shall use reasonable, best efforts to ensure that at least two members of each orchestra and/or substitutes for the Associate conductor are familiar with the score and are competent to fill-in for the Associate Conductor. Only a musician who has learned the score and who has the ability to conduct shall be eligible to receive an Associate Conductor premium."

2. Article V Minimums
The parties recognize that live music is essential to the Broadway musical experience. This Article is the contractual embodiment of that commitment.

a. The following minimum number of musicians (including leader) shall be employed at the following theatres:

Broadway, Minskoff, St. James and Marquis—19
Majestic, Palace, Lunt-Fontanne, Imperial, Gershwin, Shubert and Winter Garden—18
Neil Simon, Martin Beck and Richard Rodgers—14
Virginia and Broadhurst—12
Barrymore, Music Box and Plymouth—9
Brooks Atkinson, O'Neill and Royale—8
Longacre and Nederlander—4
Ambassador, Belasco, Booth, Circle in the Square, Cort, Golden, Walther Kerr and Lyceum—3.

b. The following minimum number of musicians (including leader) shall be employed for productions by a League producer at the New Amsterdam Theatre or The Ford Center for The Performing Arts—19.

c. The following minimum number of musicians (including leader) shall be employed for productions by BVTVI at the New Amsterdam Theatre and for productions by MRI at the Ford Center for The Performing Arts—19.

d. The following minimum number of musicians (including leader) shall be employed at any new legitimate theatre or venue—the number set forth above for a similar theatre but no more than 19.

e. The minimum provisions set forth in paragraphs a—d above shall survive the expiration of this agreement and shall remain in effect until March 4, 2013

f. Paragraph D shall be replaced by the following: "In the event that a revival is presented in a Broadway theatre, the minimum number of musicians to be employed shall be the number scored for the original Broadway production or the minimum of the theatre in which the revival performs, whichever is less."

g. Paragraph E, (paragraphs 1 through 7), shall be replaced by Attachment A.

h. The minimums in effect as of the expiration date of the prior agreements shall continue to apply to all shows scheduled to open before the cutoff date for Tony eligibility (currently May 6, 2003) or May 31, 2003, whichever comes first.

3. Article VI Non-Legitimate Attractions

Article A shall be clarified as follows: "For special non-legitimate theatrical attractions (e.g., any production without a book). . . ."

4. Article XIII Section I Health and Safety

The current language shall be replaced by Attachment B.

5. Article II.F. Just Cause

Effective after the eighth service, no musician may be dismissed except for just cause. The Employer/Producer shall have the right to request extensions of this period, which the Union shall not unreasonably deny.

6. Article VIII.K. Substitution

Modify the second sentence of Section 5(a) to provide that: "For purposes of this paragraph, the determination of what instruments shall be grouped to form each section shall be made separately for each show by the Conductor, Local 802 and the Employer/Producer."

7. Ratification:

Attachment A

The following replaces Article V Section E. In addition, the last two sentences of Article IX Section A are eliminated.

In the event that the Employer/Producer believes that there are demonstrable reasons for a musical production (including a revival) to be presented with an orchestra composed of fewer musicians than the minimum required for the theatre in which the production is to be presented, the Employer/Producer shall so advise the Union in writing as soon as possible but in no event later than the date upon which the Orchestrator's contract for the Broadway production is filed with the Union. In such event, the issue shall be promptly submitted to a Committee consisting of two (2) members from the League, two (2) members from the union and, depending upon availability, either one (1) or three (3) of the following "neutral" persons on a rotating basis: Sargent Aborn, Theodore S. Chapin, Zelda Fischandler, Robert Ferguson, Freddie Gershon, Jane Hermann, Harvey Lichtenstein, Joseph Melillo, and Victoria Traube.

Within a reasonable time after ratification, the Union may object to one or more of these proposed neutrals, after which the employers may add an equal number to replace them. The Union may also propose names, to which the employers may object pursuant to the same procedure, which shall continue until all names are agreed. No person who has a business or personal relationship with either of the parties shall be permitted to serve as a neutral if that relationship makes it impossible for him or her to function as a neutral. Additional mutually agreed upon neutral persons may be added to this list. If either party hereto objects to the appointment of one of the above named neutrals for a particular application based upon an alleged business or personal relationship as set forth above, that neutral shall be recused, and the next neutral in line shall serve in his/her stead for that application.

The Committee shall meet as promptly as possible, but in no event later than seven (7) calendar days after the Union's receipt of the aforesaid written notice from the Employer/Producer. The Employer/Producer, the Union, and/or any member of the Committee may call witnesses and present any evidence in support of their position as they see fit. The Committee shall render a written decision explaining in detail the basis for its conclusions within forty-eight (48) hours after the submission of the parties' positions. Each Committee member shall have one vote by secret ballot, and a majority vote shall prevail. In the event that the Employer/Producer or the Union does not agree with the Committee's determination, either party may submit the matter to binding arbitration before an arbitrator selected pursuant to the Voluntary Labor Arbitration rules of the American Arbitration Association. Members of the Committee may not be called as witnesses at the arbitration.

The Committee shall decide the issue based primarily on artistic considerations. If a production meets the criteria set forth in any of the following categories it shall qualify as a Special Situation and shall be permitted to perform with the requested smaller orchestra. The criteria for determining whether a production calls for a smaller orchestra are: (i) the musical concept expressed by the composer and/or orchestrator; (ii) whether the production is of a definable musical genre different from a traditional Broadway musical; (iii) the production concept expressed by the director and/or choreographer; and/or (iv) whether the production re-creates a pre-existing size band or band's sound (on or offstage).

Other considerations which shall be taken into account but which would not necessarily be determinative include but are not limited to: whether the show was previously presented with a smaller orchestra in a production of a professional caliber comparable to Broadway (*e.g.* London's West End), or whether the production was required to book a theatre with a minimum higher than the intended number of musicians due to change of theatre. A production which meets the criteria set forth in this paragraph may be denied Special Situation status only for demonstrable reasons.

The following are examples of productions that would call for a smaller orchestra under this provision and that may be cited by the Committee for that purpose: *Rent (1996); Five Guys Named Moe (1992); Ain't Misbehavin' (1978); Chicago (1975; 1996); The Best Little Whorehouse in Texas (1977); Buddy (1990); The Who's Tommy (1993); Candide (1973); Hairspray (2002); Smokey Joe's Cafe (1994); Mamma Mia! (2001); Seussical (2000); Aida (2000); Urban Cowboy (2003); Jelly's Last Jam (1992); Civil War (1999); On The Town (1998); and Little Shop of Horrors (2003).*

If a Special Situations request is denied or granted in part, the production shall utilize playing musicians up to at least the applicable minimum, or the number of playing musicians determined pursuant to the procedures set forth above, and shall not subsequently assign musician duties to actors, singers or stage personnel for the purpose of satisfying the applicable house minimum.

Once it has reached a decision, the Committee shall retain jurisdiction to consider any appropriate matters concerning, for example, either the implementation of its decision or any change in concept of the production at issue, which, inter alia, might lead to a reconsideration of its prior decision.

Attachment B

Article XIII Section I.   Health and Safety

The Employer/Producer shall make best efforts to provide a safe workplace. Any workplace hazard will be addressed by the Employer/Producer as expeditiously as possible. The Employer/Producer agrees to continue to comply with all applicable federal, New York State and New York City health and safety laws and regulations.

1. Prototype Productions

The following prototype studies involving sound levels and smoke and fog abatement proved to be successful:

High Society at the St. James for sound control

Les Misérables at the Imperial for glycol smoke/fog effects

The Phantom of the Opera at the Majestic for dry ice smoke/fog effects.

The parties recognize, however, that the combined effect of production, theatre and effect may be different for every show and that a remedy for a problem for one theatre or production may not apply to another. The procedure set forth below shall therefore apply to all current and future productions.

2. Current and Future Productions

a. The Employer/Producer agrees to notify the Union if smoke, fog, and/ or pyrotechnics are scheduled to be used. Such notification shall be given, in writing, as soon as the Employer/Producer makes the decision to use these materials. If the Union requests a meeting, it will be scheduled within a reasonable time and shall include representative(s) of Local 802, representative(s) of the Employer/Producer, and representatives(s) of the League at which meeting the parties will discuss any planned special effects such as smoke/fog and /or pyrotechnics and /or any other health and safety problem that either party feels might arise in the production.

The Employer/Producer agrees that as soon as technical decisions regarding sound are made and before the orchestra pit for a new production has been set up, there shall be a meeting that includes representative(s) of Local 802, representative(s) of the Employer/Producer, and representative(s) of the League. The Music Director/Conductor, Sound Designer, and musicians may participate at the request of either party. At such meeting the parties will discuss any changes made or contemplated in the size and shape of the pit, sound design and related issues of amplification and potential problems with space and/or sound levels. At this meeting the parties shall attempt to forestall problems from occurring.

The Union and Employer/Producer may jointly agree to engage consultants to advise them with the cost thereof shared equally by the Employer/Producer and Local 802. If the matter remains unresolved forty-five (45) days after official opening, the parties shall, upon the written request of the Union, invoke the procedure outlined below.

b. Local 802 and the League shall establish a standing Committee, consisting of two (2) persons from each side, to review, on a show by show basis, the resolution of any complaints by the Union relating to decibel levels in the orchestra performance area, temperature levels, drafts, and the like, including the use of smoke, fog, and/or pyrotechnics. The Committee shall investigate and evaluate such complaints and, where appropriate, recommend solutions that seek to maintain a healthy workplace. The Committee shall meet within seven (7) days of any written complaint, and, where warranted, authorize either the implementation of appropriate remedial techniques or devices which have been successfully utilized at other theatres or the use of other techniques or devices if the conditions of a production so require. The Committee shall be authorized to engage consultants and/or to provide for appropriate testing, sampling or monitoring, if necessary to advise the Committee. In its deliberations, the Committee may consider, in addition to federal, state or city health and safety regulations, other applicable health standards. The costs thereof shall be shared equally by the Employer/Producer and Local 802. If the Committee cannot agree upon a solution after appropriate deliberations, either party may request final and binding arbitration before a panel of experts consisting of two (2) persons designated by the Union, two (2) persons designated by the League and one (1) person designated by these four, who shall be a qualified professional in the area under consideration. Should the parties disagree on the selection of the fifth member, the procedures of the American Arbitration Association shall be utilized to select the fifth member from a list of qualified professionals submitted by each party. The cost of the arbitration shall be shared equally by the parties. In considering this matter, it shall be understood that every show and every theatre may be different and that a remedy for a problem at one theatre may not necessarily apply to another. Neither the Committee nor the arbitrator may affect or alter audience seating, number of instruments, scenic elements of the show (other than smoke, fog, pyrotechnics that enter orchestra performing areas) or architectural features of the theatres. Once an agreement is reached or a determination is made by an arbitrator, the resolution of the complaint shall be implemented as expeditiously as possible. The cost of any remedial measures shall be paid by the Employer/Producer.

Any claimed violation of the procedures outlined in this paragraph 2(b) shall be submitted to the expedited arbitration procedures of the American Arbitration Association.

c. The Employer/Producer shall conduct Right to Know sessions for musicians prior to the first public performance to make them aware of any substances to which they might be exposed in the course of their work. Such sessions shall be scheduled contiguous to a rehearsal and shall not be compensated time. The Employer/Producer shall also provide to Local 802 a copy of Material Safety Data Sheets (MSDS).

3. Review and Readjustment

No initial determination of a successful resolution of a problem shall preclude the review and readjustment, if necessary, in accordance with the procedure set forth in 2(b) above, of any such prior resolution if there are changes in the sound levels or amount or type of smoke, fog and/or pyrotechnics.

APPENDIX B

1. Contractor—Article II, p. 2
   a. The employer shall have the option of engaging a contractor who is not a playing musician and who is not covered by the contract.
   b. If the employer chooses to engage a playing musician as the contractor, such musician shall receive a premium payment of $200 per week during the term of this agreement.

2. Cuts List—Article II B, p. 2
   Clarify language to provide that employer may reduce the number of musicians to the minimum at any time without any future conditions so long as the minimum number of musicians is employed in the orchestra.

3. Dismissal—Article II, p.3
   Paragraph F shall apply as of the official opening.

4. Associate Conductor, Article III C. p. 5
   a. There shall be no move-up payment to another musician if the Associate Conductor is called upon to conduct.
   b. There shall be no Associate Conductor payment to another musician when the Associate Conductor is absent.
   c. The Associate Conductor payment shall be frozen for the term of this agreement at the current dollar level.

5. Librarian—Article III D, p.5
   The Librarian payment shall apply through the official opening and only thereafter when the Librarian function is performed.
   The Librarian payment shall be frozen for the term of this agreement at the current dollar level.

6. Hiatus Layoff—Article III E, p. 5
If a layoff occurs between an out of town pre-Broadway try out and the New York opening of more than two but less than six weeks, the musicians will be paid 50% scale salary during the period of such layoff. If the layoff is six weeks or more, the Employer shall not be obligated to make any weekly payments and neither party shall have any further obligation to the other.

7. Payments—Article III.I. p. 7
Incremental and percentage payments shall not be made during rehearsals and auditions when less than the full orchestra is employed.

8. Rehearsal Conditions—Article IV 1A. p. 7
Amend to read: "The musicians and the Union shall receive not less than seven (7) days prior notice of the date of the first reading rehearsal as well as the starting time of all scheduled rehearsals, except during the final seven days of rehearsal prior to the day of the first paid public performance, the starting time of scheduled rehearsals may be changed upon 12 hours notice. Musicians may not send substitutes to rehearsals during this period."

9. Rehearsal Conditions—Article IV 1 A1, p. 7
Delete last sentence of paragraph, i.e. "Once the rehearsals have commenced. . . . such hiatus."

10. Minimums—Article V A, 12.11

Broadway, Majestic, Palace, Lunt-Fontanne, Gershwin, Imperial, Marquis, Minskoff, St. James, Shubert and Winter Garden	24
Neil Simon and Richard Rodgers	18
Martin Beck	14
Broadhurst and Virginia	12
Barrymore, Brooks Atkinson, Music Box, Eugene O'Neill Plymouth and Royale	7
Longacre, Nederlander, Ambassador, Belasco, Booth, Cort, Golden, Walter Kerr, and Lyceum	3

Delete Circle in the Square and Biltmore from the list.

11. Seventh Consecutive Day, Article VII B, p. 15
Time and one-half (1 ½) premium is to be paid to the musician who plays on the seventh consecutive day provided the musician has performed services on the previous six days.

12. Sunday Premium, Article VIII D, p. 15
Delete time and one-half premium for second Sunday performance.

13. Third Performance Premium, Article VIII E, p. 15
The third performance premium shall only be paid to musicians who actually play three performances on one day.

14. Substitutions Article VIII K, p. 16
Commencing eight performances after the official opening, the Producer shall have the right to terminate the employment of any musician who has been replaced by a substitute more than 25% of the performances within each period of 48 consecutive performances, unless ill, on vacation, or on approved leave of absence.

15. Reporting Time, Article VIII L. p. 19
All musicians shall be present at the theatre 15 minutes prior to curtain and shall be in place, properly attired and ready to play at the start of the performance.

16. First Chair Trumpet Premium, Article IX E, p. 19
Delete paragraph E

17. Pension, Article XV, p. 25
To the extent the musicians allocable share of the .045 monies exceed the contractually required pension contribution, such excess shall be applied as follows:
   a. to offset health and hospitalization contributions
   b. to offset sick pay contributions
   c. to offset any pension contribution required to be made on behalf of Local 802 members on a road tour of the production.

Increase the contract percentage from 5% to 10%.

18. Most Favored Nations, Article XX, p. 28
In the event Local 802 grants more favorable terms and conditions to any employer employing musicians in a theatrical production on Broadway, then, in such more favorable terms and conditions shall also be granted to employers under this agreement and this agreement shall be deemed amended accordingly.

19. Schedule A. Doubles p. 35
The rate for doubles shall be fixed for the term of the agreement at the current rate: First Double—$137.50; Each additional double—$68.75.

20. Promotions, Publicity and Commercials

    a. <u>B-Roll Footage—No Payment Required</u>—B-Roll footage may be used without additional compensation for the following uses:

    <u>Press Reels</u>: Producer can use clips of up to a total of three minutes of performance and/or rehearsal footage (of which no continuous sequence shall exceed 30 seconds) for each production included on the Press Reel.

    <u>Web Sites</u>: Up to a total of three minutes of rehearsal and/or performance footage (of which no continuous sequence shall exceed 30 seconds) may be used either in a directory or multiple Broadway show format (i.e. "I Love New York" format) or by an individual Producer on behalf of a particular show or group of shows. Neither merchandise promotion nor ticket sale information shall be presented on the same "page" as the foregoing, but may be presented on a separate "page." However, the page containing B-Roll may indicate how to get to the page which does have information about merchandise or tickets. It is also understood that there may be no promotion of any other product(s) on the "page" whether the B-Roll footage will be seen without Local 802's prior written consent.

    <u>News and Current Affairs Programs</u>: Producer can use clips for up to three minutes in total time on each such show so long as the film or tape does not contain an entire number.

    <u>Entertainment Talk Shows</u>: Producer can use clips for up to three minutes as part of an interview.

    b. The Producer may be permitted to cut several commercials from the original B-Roll or commercial footage without any additional session payment.

    c. <u>Group Sales and Industry Promotions</u>: When a musician is employed for group sales or industry promotion, the musician shall be paid at the rehearsal hourly rate of pay for a minimum of two hours.

21. Schedule B proposals will be submitted at a later date.

22. The Employers reserve the right to add to, modify or delete any proposal.

APPENDIX C

THEATRE STATISTICS AND MINIMUMS: FOR CONTRACTS EXPIRING 1993–2013

Theatre	Seats	Owner	1993	1998	2003	2013
Al Hirschfeld	1437	Jujamcyn	16	16	16	14
Ambassador	1125	Shubert	9	3	3	3
Belasco	1018	Shubert	9	3	3	3
Biltmore	650	Manhattan Theatre Club	9	3	3	3
Booth	785	Shubert	6	3	3	3
Broadhurst	1186	Shubert	15	15	15	12
Broadway	1752	Shubert	26	26	26	19
Brooks Atkinson	1044	Nederlander	9	9	9	8
Cadillac Winter Garden	1513	Shubert	25	24	24	18
Circle in the Square	623	N/A	6	3	3	3
Cort	1084	Shubert	9	3	3	3
Ethel Barrymore	1096	Shubert	9	9	9	9
Eugene O'Neill	1108	Jujamcyn	9	9	9	8
Ford Center	1813	Clear Channel	N/A	24	24	19
Gershwin	1933	Nederlander	24	24	24	18
Imperial	1421	Shubert	26	24	24	18
John Golden	805	Shubert	6	3	3	3
Longacre	1096	Shubert	9	5	5	4
Lunt-Fontanne	1475	Nederlander	26	25	25	18
Lyceum	924	Shubert	9	3	3	3
Majestic	1655	Shubert	26	26	26	18

continued

continued

Theatre	Seats	Owner	1993	1998	2003	2013
Marquis	1604	Nederlander	24	24	24	19
Minskoff	1710	Nederlander	24	24	24	19
Music Box	1010	Shubert*	9	9	9	9
Nederlander	1203	Nederlander	16	5	5	4
Neil Simon	1297	Nederlander	20	20	20	14
New Amsterdam	1747	Disney	N/A	24	24	19
Palace	1784	Nederlander	26	25	25	18
Plymouth	1079	Shubert	9	9	9	9
Richard Rogers	1368	Nederlander	25	24	24	14
Royale	1521	Shubert	9	9	9	8
Shubert	1524	Shubert	26	24	24	18
St. James	1623	Jujamcyn	25	24	24	19
Virginia	1275	Jujamcyn	16	16	16	12
Walter Kerr	947	Jujamcyn	6	3	3	3
Total			518	500	500	392

*The estate of Irving Berlin also is a part owner of the Music Box Theatre.
Source: <http://www.livebroadway.com/theaters_broadway.html and the "Memorandum Of Agreement.

APPENDIX D

ORCHESTRA COSTS FOR THE WEEK OF JANUARY 5, 2003

Production	Weekly Gross	Avg. Ticket Price	Weekly Orchestra Cost (Incl. Benefits)	Orchestra Cost As A Portion of Avg. Ticket
42nd Street	$799,563	$64.56	$45,810	$3.70
Aida	$712,626	$67.79	$32,620	$3.10
Beauty and Beast	$785,259	$70.55	$48,720	$4.38
Cabaret	$439,871	$65.13	$11,040	$1.63
Chicago	$644,009	$68.22	$27,410	$2.90
Dance*Vampires	$476,979	$58.97	$50,230	$6.21
Flower Drum Song	$420,041	$68.03	$26,760	$5.95
Hairspray	$1,025,021	$88.67	$40,080	$3.47
Imaginary Friends	$159,560	$61.44	$11,620	$4.47
La Boheme	$1,013,328	$77.44	$55,320	$4.23
Les Misérables	$854,775	$76.96	$51,140	$4.60
Mamma Mia!	$1,099,957	$90.24	$22,320	$1.83
Man of La Mancha	$663,414	$73.35	$30,550	$3.38
Movin' Out	$751,690	$83.32	$21,450	$2.38
Oklahoma!	$532,954	$66.66	$48,855	$6.11
Rent	$482,924	$57.08	$12,251	$1.45
The Lion King	$1,272,925	$87.64	$48,890	$3.37
The Phantom of the Opera	$789,567	$67.20	$50,970	$4.34
The Producers	$1,130,850	$84.35	$47,060	$3.51
Thoroughly*Millie	$790,637	$73.78	$48,260	$4.50
Urinetown	$347,166	$70.98	$10,960	$2.24
Total	$15,193,116		$742,316	

Source: www.savelivebroadway.com

Notes

NOTES TO CHAPTER 1

1. Board of Governors of the Federal Reserve System, "Flow of Funds Accounts of the United States," 1995–2000 and 1965–1974; The US Census <http://www.census.gov/population/estimates/nation/popclockest.txt>; The Bureau of Labor Statistics <http://www.bls.gov> and the author's own calculations.
2. Society-wide collective bargaining is known as 'social bargaining' (Edwards and Podgursky).
3. Throughout history there have been challenges to the existing social/economic order; however, the challenges have typically been on the "political fringe" and consequently dismissed (Mantsios 59–62).
4. Firms like Gene Levine Associates publish handbooks and offer consulting services to ensure that firms remain "union free." This firm's "number one maxim of union avoidance is, 'you can't lose an election you don't have'" (Gene Levine).
5. An example of this is how the Saturn automobile was produced. Originally, workers (union members) participated in production decisions. However, Saturn has since returned to traditional production methods.
6. The term "communism" used in this book needs to be clearly distinguished from the "Communism" practiced in the USSR for almost a century. The former advocates the collective appropriation and distribution of surplus, the latter does not. For a detailed analysis of the USSR and its "Communism" see *Class Theory and History*, by Stephen Resnick and Richard Wolff, 2002.
7. Any process that does not include the production, appropriation, and/or distribution of surplus is considered a non-class process within the NMCA framework; such non-class processes can be political, cultural, natural, economic, or any combination of the four.
8. Of course, law or edict might require some surplus distributions. For example, a communist enterprises like any other enterprise would be required by law to pay taxes.
9. The word 'producer' assumes multiple meanings within NMCA methodology, therefore when referring to the Broadway Producer qua capitalist, the word 'Producer' is capitalized throughout the book. This distinction is necessary to differentiate between other types of producers, for example a worker as a surplus value producer.

NOTES TO CHAPTER 2

1. Fixed royalties are 14% of the musicals' expenditures. The figure cited here includes royalty payments to particular workers who have individually

negotiated this benefit into their personal contracts (not in collective bargaining agreements). For example, many stars receive royalties because of their 'star appeal' and the idea that their notoriety will increase audience attendance and thereby increase the profitability of the show. The Broadway musicians' collective bargaining agreement sets only minimum 'scale' wages and benefits. Workers are free to negotiate terms and agreements over and above the minimum scale wage with their employers, and this excess payment may be in the form of a royalty.

2. This book is a specific inquiry into the Broadway musicians' class positions and how they might improve their working situation by challenging these positions. Therefore, the legal structure of the both types of firms is capitalist, whether corporate, like Disney and Clear Channel, or Limited Liability Company, as most of the other Producers opt for, does not have a direct effect on the class-transformation prototype that will be discussed in Chapter 4.

3. As well as other workers such as the actors.

4. The exceptions are Disney and Clear Channel as mentioned above.

5. The Producer may or may not invest his/her own personal funds. In the NMCA methodology, investment, ownership, or power does not define the capitalist; surplus value appropriation does. As will be discussed in Chapter 4, if the Producer invests his/her own personal funds, then s/he will receive a subsumed class payment in the form of a 'royalty' for this investment.

6. The legal definition of net profits here is qualitatively different than the Marxian definition of net profits. The discussion here is simply to highlight a payment the Producers are legally bound to make to secure their conditions of existence as capitalist. As will be discussed below, the payment(s) made to investors, is a subsumed class payment made by the Producer from the surplus value s/he appropriates.

7. Although, the Producer is the first recipient of the gross profits, s/he must make legally necessary payments to certain constituents, the investors as mentioned here for example.

8. The "managing member" is discussed directly below.

9. The Producer receives 50% for his position as Producer, and s/he could possibly receive an additional payment if s/he is an investor as well.

10. In various discussions below, I will discern between which of these payments are fundamental class payments and which payments are from the surplus value, i.e., subsumed class payments.

11. This estimate includes dramatic plays as well as musicals.

12. The managing member may consist of one or more persons, or co-Producers. Whether the capitalist is an individual or a group of individuals, such as a Board of Directors, does not change the class analysis.

13. "'Gross receipts' shall mean all sums derived by the Company from the exploitation or turning to account of its rights in the Play [Musical] (which shall be acquired from the Managing Member upon formation of the Company) including all proceeds derived by the Company from the liquidation of the physical production of the Play [Musical] at the conclusion of the run thereof, and from the return of bonds and other recoverable items included in the Production Expenses" (D. Farber, *Producing Theatre* 435–6).

14. Sums include but are not limited to: necessary operating expenses, theatre rents, royalty payments, wages, etc. Of course, many of these payments are contractual, whether in the form of a lease, contract, or collective bargaining agreement, but it is the Managing Member who makes the final decision and it is s/he alone can decide to close a show.

15. A complete list of the theatres and number of seats is provided in Appendix C.
16. Theatre owners prefer "license agreements" to traditional tenant/landlord leases to avoid the many legal constraints associated with the leases ((D. Farber, *Producing Theatre* 209).
17. As previously mentioned, the Producer(s) may also own the theatre. Each theatre owner is or has been the Producer of one or more musical(s).
18. A sample "Theatre License Agreement" can be found in Appendix K, pages 485–499 of D. Farber, *Producing Theatre.*
19. See Appendix C, "Theatre Statistics and Minimums."
20. "The term legitimate refers in general to what contracts call 'first-class' shows in 'first-class' theatres" (Rosenberg 8). This book includes only "legitimate" productions.
21. Each group of workers is covered by a collective bargaining agreement with their respective unions.
22. A "side-musician" is one who does not occupy the position of conductor or associate conductor.
23. Formally the "The League American Theatres and Producers."
24. When Disney first entered the Broadway industry, it joined the League; however, in 1997, Disney rescinded its membership.
25. http://www.broadwayleague.com/index.php?url_identifer=membership-1
26. This is true in most capitalist enterprises. That is, the workers cooperate and work collectively in the capitalist mode of production. Cooperation/collectivity does not, however, imply the class structure of the enterprise.
27. Local 802 defines a musician as full time if they work on Broadway more than 20 hours in a calendar year.
28. This assumes that each Broadway theatre houses a musical and that the minimum number of musicians as stipulated in the collective bargaining agreement is utilized in each instance.
29. Article 8(K), "Substitutions."
30. Article V. E, "Special Situations."
31. In a March 2003 interview with Local 802 president, Bill Moriarity, he stated that he was coerced into accepting a negotiated minimum by the mediator assigned by Mayor Bloomberg. Had the union not moved on this issue, the League would have filed an Unfair Labor Practice with the National Labor Relations Board. The musicians were discontented with the result, but the collective bargaining agreement was ratified which ended the four-day strike. In a subsequent May 4, 2003 interview with Music Coordinator, Seymour 'Red' Press, Mr. Press said that it is his belief that the union lost the strike because it decreased the minimums.
32. Appendix D "Orchestra Costs."
33. Article VIII.A, "Work Week."
34. If the musician plays a second or more unrelated instrument(s), the compensation for each subsequent instrument is 6.25% of his/her basic wage.
35. A costume is any garb that is other than all black clothing or a tuxedo.
36. This premium was negotiated to deter the use of electronic instruments in that they take the place of musicians. A synthesizer could (although some would question the quality) take the place of an entire philharmonic of 106 musicians.
37. Carpal tunnel syndrome as well as other concerns of the Broadway musicians will be discussed in Chapters 3 and 5.
38. The conductor receives a 75% premium over scale and the associate conductor receives 30%.

39. While the relative power of the conductor may not be explicitly stated in the collective bargaining agreement, some prominent conductors wield considerable power and authority over hiring, firing, and other traditional supervisory functions.
40. Article VIII.K.(2), "Substitutions."
41. According to the National Labor Relations Act, Section 2(11): " The term 'supervisor' means any individual having authority, in the interest of the employer, to hire, transfer, suspend, lay off, recall, promote, discharge, assign, reward, or discipline other employees, or responsibly to direct them, or to adjust their grievances, or effectively to recommend such action, if in connection with the foregoing the exercise of such authority is not of a merely routine or clerical nature, but requires the use of independent judgment."
42. There is no contractual requirement for the MD position.
43. Often the MC is referred to as the "contractor," but because s/he is a playing musician, s/he is known as the "designated contractor" or the "in-house contractor," as required by the collective bargaining agreement. To simplify the discussion it is helpful to make a clear distinction between the two positions.
44. Article II.A "Hiring Practices."
45. The MC may indeed be an employee of the theatre owner if that same person is a playing musician in the orchestra. For example, Red Press is the MC for the current Broadway musical "Chicago." Mr. Press also plays the clarinet in the same show. For his role as MC he is an employee of the Producer and is paid from the Producer's payroll. For his role as side-musician, he is an employee of the theatre owner and receives his salary from the owner. Also the MC is simultaneously a worker and his own supervisor.
46. The issue of "minimum" staffing for musicians was detailed above in the subsection "Workers."
47. The MC's position will be discussed in greater detail below.
48. When asked about retirement (May 4, 2003), Mr. Press responded in the negative. However, he did say that he is no longer soliciting MC type work; but if something interesting comes his way, he will not decline.
49. As mentioned above, for the current production of "Chicago," Mr. Press is simultaneously the MC, the in-house contractor, and the reeds player.
50. MC salaries are confidential thus I was not able to obtain information regarding the exact payments made to each particular MC. However, in one off the record discussion with newcomer MC Michael Keller, he did think that he needed to give Producers a 'bargain price' for his services simply to have access to the job.
51. To my knowledge, no MC has ever held the position as a Producer of a Broadway musical. Doing so might jeopardize his position as a playing musician within or without Broadway.
52. All five Broadway music coordinators are white men. This in itself might intimate the possibility of discriminatory practices. I will address this assertion below.
53. Evidence of progressive discipline might be in the form of oral and written warnings of a particular infraction in the musician's personnel file.
54. According to Mr. Seymour Press in an interview on May 4, 2003, musicians are rarely fired. In fact, he further stated, in his long history of working and acting as a Music Coordinator on Broadway for almost 50 years, Mr. Press recalls firing only four musicians, two of whom were rehired after winning a union grievance. However, Mr. Press also stated that he would never hire any of the four again.
55. Article I.A. "Union Security and Dues Checkoff [sic]."

56. The collective bargaining agreement covers not only the groups mentioned here, it also covers Music Preparation personnel, such as orchestrators and copyists. This book excludes Music Preparation personnel and its focus will be entirely on the playing (orchestra pit) musicians including the conductors.

57. High union density rates typically assume that the workers in that particular enterprise have a level of solidarity that wields them relative power vis-à-vis their employers. However, even with a 100% union density rate, historically, the Broadway theatre personnel have endured extremely harsh working conditions. And now even with the high unionization rates, many of these conditions remain; this is the basic impetus for this book. Unlike other industries, in which workers toil for wages and do not particularly have an affinity for their employments, this is not so with musicians and actors who long to get that 'big break' that participating on Broadway provides.

58. For example, Local 802 musicians have committees that include the theatre committee, the club date musicians' committee, the Musical Directors' committee, the hotel musicians' committee, the jazz musicians' committee and the symphony orchestra members' committee.

59. There is a definite power relationship that comes into play with regard to the MC and the Conductor. For example, if the MC is John Miller and there is a novice conductor, then Miller's decisions prevail.

NOTES TO CHAPTER 3

1. The musicians are particularly concerned about being consulted about creative issues.

2. Worker participation/voice and job security are deemed non-economic issues—though they are unquestionably economic to Marxists. Unions' typically deem non-economic issues peripheral. For example, when teaching collective bargaining to union members, labor educators stress the importance of leaving the primary economic issues of wages and benefits until the end of negotiations and to negotiate the more 'mundane' issues of working conditions at the outset.

3. As mentioned in Chapter 2, Local 802's President Bill Moriarity is of the same philosophy. He too gives primacy in bargaining to wages and benefits, i.e. the 'economic' issues.

4. In general, worker participation schemes are limited in most union proposals. More typically, they are completely nonexistent.

5. As will become evident below, issues of safety and health, worker participation, and job security are indeed economic concerns. The perception that these issues are 'non-economic' is critical to this analysis and the proposed prototype in Chapter 4.

6. Many musicians have complained about the filth in the orchestra pits. Indeed, in the collective bargaining agreement there is the stipulation in article XIII.A that "[l]ocker rooms and playing areas shall be cleaned daily." Most pits are not even cleaned weekly. For example, there were anonymous grievances by members of the "Phantom of the Opera" orchestra of rat feces in the orchestra pit.

7. Please refer to chapter 2 for a discussion of the threat to a Broadway musician's career if s/he is not complacent.

8. Article IV.H. "Working Conditions."

9. Local 802 did investigate multiple complaints regarding extreme sound levels. Local 802 hired an industrial hygienist who measured decibel

levels. Her reports are discussed below in the section entitled "Excessive Sound Levels."

10. I am the union representative who experienced this.

11. Article XIII.I.1.a.

12. Buena Vista Theatrical Inc. (Disney) made some special effects changes prior to the 1998 collective bargaining agreement at "Beauty and the Beast." The modifications, however, were not sufficient in reducing the negative health effects the musicians encountered. Furthermore, when noise levels were deemed extreme by testing completed by consultants hired by the musicians' union, some pit modifications were made. Again, however, these modifications rarely were adequate solutions.

13. Dr. Jacqueline Moline in a private conversation with me stated that the jerry-rigged respiratory devices used by the musicians could indeed exacerbate any negative health affects from the particulates.

14. On more than one occasion, health professionals cautioned musicians about wearing ergonomically incorrect respirators and ear protection devices.

15. Article XIII Section I. "Health and Safety."

16. While the scenery might not be problematic for the musicians, this is not the case for the actors. Much of the latest scenery often requires the actors to perform under dangerous conditions, such as performing high above the stage or on a sharp incline. The Actors' Equity collective bargaining agreement, the union contract that covers all of the actors on Broadway, requires premium pay for actors who work under these conditions.

17. Some would argue that the considerable scenery expenditures are necessary to the musical's success, which thereby increases the probability of longer employment for the musicians. The Producers make this argument; otherwise they would not incur the expenditures.

18. Dry ice is not without its own set of dangers. "Dry ice is one of the earliest types of materials used to create fog effects. Dry ice is frozen carbon dioxide, and when exposed to air it converts directly from a solid to a gas. The cold gas causes moisture to condense into a thick, low-lying fog. Dry ice is the safest way to generate fog except in enclosed spaces where the carbon dioxide can accumulate and reduce the oxygen concentration in the air. This could cause asphyxiation if the oxygen concentration falls below 19.5%. There would also be a hazard if someone were lying down in the dry ice fog" (AOL®Hometown 1).

19. Associated Musicians of Greater NY, Local 802, Contract Survey, November 17, 1997.

20. While only a few documented cases, there have been complaints by audience members of foul smells and minor respiratory irritation such as coughing.

21. The Broadway Actors' union, "Actors' Equity' (AE) and the League commissioned the Department of Community and Preventive Medicine Mount Sinai School of Medicine and ENVIRON International Corporation a three year study released on June 6, 2000 entitled "Health Effects Evaluation of Theatrical Smoke, Haze, and Pyrotechnics." The study "concluded that Actors are at risk when exposed to 'elevated or peak levels of glycol smoke and mineral oil.'" Subsequently, AE and the League agreed to set limitations on the use of smoke and fog which may have positive affects to the Broadway musicians as well. See: http://www.actorsequity.org/TheatreNews/smokefog_0501.html.

22. I have documentation from various health care professionals to support these allegations. I have also interviewed both doctors and the musicians as well as made my own observations.

23. Many musicians have reported to me and Local 802 that they are fearful of John Miller's reputation for not hiring or rehiring any musician who does not

conform. As discussed in the previous chapter, the MC hires orchestras for Broadway musicals and the relationship between the musician and the MC is often tenuous in the sense that, if the musicians raise issues, they might not be hired for 'the next show,' giving the MC a quite powerful position vis-à-vis the musicians. This is of particular importance on Broadway because of the ephemeral lifespan of most shows; it is therefore imperative for their own job security that musicians maintain a subservient relationship to the MC. This is particularly true in the case of John Miller who is currently Broadway's most prolific MC; of the 18 Broadway musicals open in July 2004, Producers selected Miller as the MC for nine shows or 50%.

24. See Appendix A "2003 Memorandum of Agreement."
25. 2003 Memorandum of Agreement, Attachment B.1 "Prototype Productions."
26. The Producers made this argument repeatedly during the 1998 negotiations.
27. Historically, Broadway orchestra pits were in front of the stage, set just a bit lower than the foot it so that the musicians were seen by the audience; the musicians' heads were just below stage level. Now, orchestra pits are underneath the stage and all the audience can see is the conductor's head. Additionally, only a small opening now exists between the stage and the audience—and this opening is continually decreasing, thus enclosing the pit so that sounds reverberate in them. The reason for this change is due to the Producers' pursuit of increased profits. Enclosure of the pits has made room for additional audience seats at the usual rate of $100 or more per seat in the orchestra section.
28. "Sound levels are measured in units of decibels (dB). In measuring sound levels, instruments are used which resemble the human ear in sensitivity to noise composed of varying frequencies. The instruments measure the 'A-weighted sound level' in units called dBA." US Department of Labor, Occupational Safety and Health Administration (*Noise Control: A guide for workers and employers* 1980).
29. Even though both the League and Local 802 agreed to the special effects and sound control prototypes, the payments for these as well as any hired consultants were paid out of the Union's Sick Pay Fund. Union officials believed that it was in the best interest of their membership to make these payments, though they finance permanent structural improvements for the theatres. In the subsequent 2003 agreement, it was negotiated that the Producer/employer and the Local 802 will equally share the cost burden for such devices. See Appendix A "2003 Memorandum of Agreement."
30. According to a July 2002 article in the *Allegro*, Local 802's newsletter, David Lennon, the presiding President stated simply that "the sound treatments at both "High Society" and "Miss Saigon" were judged a success in significantly reducing sound levels and improving the overall sound of the orchestra." However, the scientific sound measurements by an authorized industrial hygienist were not performed subsequent to the installation of the sound control devices.
31. Historically, the season ran from September until the Tony Awards in May. Presently, some Broadway insiders continue to acknowledge the beginning of the 'season' after Labor Day in September; however, for some shows the season does not end with the Tonys. Show longevity (for multiple seasons) is a rather new phenomenon.
32. Carpal tunnel syndrome, a hand and wrist disorder that may cause debilitating pain and weakness in the thumb and fingers, is the most common of all injuries that result from jobs requiring repetitive motions. The incidence

of repetitive motion injuries has escalated in the last two decades—from 18 percent of all workplace maladies in 1981 to 48 percent in 1988, according to a U.S. Department of Labor study (Peiken).

33. Some researchers argue that with the introduction of the 'team' type of production, workers have more input in the work process and productivity increases. However, what we have been witnessing with the idea of 'teams' is that once productivity increases are realized, the firm then decreases the workforce, i.e., workers are terminated (Tormey).

34. Indeed, many nations that once challenged private capitalism, or at least professed to challenge it, have now embraced it, e.g. China.

35. Refer to the discussion on "Commodity Unionism" in Chapter 2.

36. Article II.H. "Hiring Practices."

37. However, during a March 2003 interview with Local 802 president, Bill Moriarity, he admitted that the clause was implemented because of one particular Producer's manipulation of certain restrictions articulated in the collective bargaining agreement. To meet the minimum requirement of orchestra pit musicians, this particular Producer would "hire" his wife, children, and other relatives who were not musicians. Furthermore, according to Moriarity, he doubts that these so-called musicians were ever paid a salary, although officially they were. The minimum requirement is in place for various reasons, but one of the principal reasons is job security for musicians. The practice of hiring non-musician relatives negates this intention.

38. As will be shown in the section in Chapter 4 entitled "Class-Transformative Agenda," it is not essential for the Broadway musicians to become the producers (capitalists) in order to eradicate their exploitation.

39. Appendix C: "Theatre Statistics and Minimums: For contracts expiring 1993–2013."

40. Appendix A, Memorandum of Agreement, 2003, "Attachment 1."

41. League, *Collective Bargaining Agreement*, Article II.F: "No musician shall be dismissed except for just cause." Most other unions venerate this specific article. Obviously it protects the musicians from being capriciously or arbitration terminated; but this article ensures more than that. Musicians are hired for the run of the show after they played in the first orchestra rehearsal. It is extremely difficult for a Broadway musician to be fired.

   Indeed, in my two and one half years as the Broadway union representative, only one musician was terminated. This particular "Cats" musician routinely disregarded many of the terms of the collective bargaining agreement, especially the overuse of substitutes. (League, *Collective Bargaining Agreement*, Article VIII.K). The Producers through the MC Mel Rodnon documented the musician's disregard of his contractual obligations. Furthermore, the musician was previously warned and received progressive discipline actions, which is atypical on Broadway. Probably due to the typically short durations of Broadway musicals, MCs and other Broadway supervisors are not particularly diligent with keeping disciplinary records or administering discipline. The MC gives the disciplinary action to the recalcitrant musician by his not rehiring the musician for subsequent musicals. *Cats* is an anomaly, in that by the time this particular musician was terminated, he had a tenure of fifteen years with the show and continually disregarded the collective bargaining agreement and warnings.

   The point is that it was almost impossible for the MC and the Producers to even terminate a musician who was so egregiously unmanageable. Therefore, Broadway musicians typically remain for the entire run of the show, except if the musician him/herself decides to quit. The Producers believed they were constrained by the provisions and/or benefits to the Broadway musicians in this article, therefore, in 2003 they insisted on its modification. Now the article states that "The Employer/Producer shall have the right to request extensions of this period, which the Union shall not unreasonably deny" (League, 2003 *Memorandum*).

42. Mulder, Catherine P. Broadway negotiation notes, 1998.
43. "The Phantom of the Opera" orchestra now only employs the minimum number (26) of musicians required at the Majestic Theatre. The Majestic's minimum requirement for "The Phantom of the Opera" reflects the requirement stated collective bargaining agreement when it opened in January 1988.
44. Not all Broadway theatres are used for musicals; for example on February 17, 2004, 19 shows were musicals, or 52% of the theatres housed musicals, while the other 42% were either vacant or housed dramatic plays. Additionally, some of these shows are not required to hire the minimum because they meet the "special situations" requirements.
45. A Virtual Orchestra is basically a synthesizer that replicates an entire orchestra's sounds.
46. Often synthesizers are used to augment the string section. That is, while there may be a small string section in the orchestra, synthesizers have the capability to give the effect of a much larger string section.
47. Gracie Mansion is the official residence of the Mayor of New York City.
48. The argument of the musicians' relative lack of importance is of concern to this project and may in fact be addressed by the prototype discussed in Chapter 4.
49. See Appendix A *Memorandum of Agreement, 2003*.
50. A Broadway Music Coordinator is a 'labor broker,' much like those in the temporary services industry. Although I do not believe the Broadway MCs receive a fee from the musicians for their services as required by many temporary services, they do however, receive payments from the Producer(s) for the entire length of the musical. Like the temporary employment industry, Broadway musicians must maintain an amicable relationship with the individual, i.e., the labor broker who is the only means of access to a job.
51. Music Coordinators are not recognized in the collective bargaining agreement. In March 2003, I asked Local 802 President Bill Moriarity about how the role and power of the MCs evolved, he replied, "musicians have always been hired by contractors [MCs]." He also said that Local 802 has never challenged the role of the MC.
52. The 1200 musicians do not hold full-time Broadway positions; many of these musicians are substitutes.

NOTES TO CHAPTER 4

1. Revolution is defined here as a change in a class position of the particular agent under investigation; more on this will be presented below.
2. For a more comprehensive discussion of NMCA see S. Resnick and R. Wolff, *Knowledge and Class*; J.K. Gibson-Graham, *The End of Capitalism (as we knew it)*; and A. Callari, S. Cullenberg and C. Biewener, *Marxism in the Postmodern Age: Confronting the New World Order*.
3. Surplus is hereby defined as the labor workers perform that is more than necessary labor "sufficient to produce the goods and services their current standard of living requires" (Resnick and Wolff, *Knowledge* 20).
4. While there are 5 distinct class processes (ancient, feudal, slave, capitalist, and communist) in NMCA, this book will only address two of them, capitalist and communist. The reason for this is because the Broadway musicians

currently work in a capitalist class structure and the proposal forthwith is a communist alternative.

5. Capitalist surplus value producers (workers) may also indeed receive a subsumed class payment from capitalist distributors. For example, a worker may own stock in a capitalist firm and thus because of his/her position as stockowner, s/he might receive a distribution of the surplus value in the form of a dividend. As will be exposed below, indeed some of the Broadway musicians receive subsumed class payments from the capitalist Producers.

6. Such as the Broadway League in the form of dues, the Theatre Owners in the form of rent, the composers and writers in the form of royalties, and the State in the form of taxes, among others.

7. "As the seller of labor power, the laborer occupies a nonclass position; as a producer of surplus value, the laborer occupies a fundamental class position" (Resnick and Wolff, *Knowledge* 151).

8. A 'productive' worker is a person who produces surplus.

9. As will be discussed below, the Producer will hold an additional subsumed class position as a recipient of the surplus value.

10. The collective bargaining agreement commencing on March 9, 1998 made this distinction explicit. In prior collective bargaining agreements the contract language simply said "Employer." Subsequently, the collective bargaining agreement language has been modified to say "Employer/Producer."

11. Refer to the section in Chapter 2 titled "The Capitalist as the 'managing member.'"

12. A "productive" worker in the NMCA framework is a worker who directly produces surplus value (Resnick and Wolff, *Knowledge* 132–141).

13. This payment is a non-class payment because it precedes the class process of the production of surplus value. Additionally, the payment in not a distribution of surplus value, in that none is produced until after the 'property' is purchased.

14. This is not to say that the productive workers are somehow more important in the production process than the workers who do not actually produce the new commodity. Indeed, capitalists would not retain the nonproductive workers if they were not necessary to secure the capitalist's conditions of existence. For example, administrative assistants are vital workers to most firms; these workers facilitate the smooth running of the enterprise. The reference here to regarding the integral nature of productive workers, is simply that these workers, in their fundamental class position as surplus value producers are precisely the people who transform the means of production into a new commodity and are therefore primary in this position.

15. The distinction of 'minimum' scale wages is made here because musicians may negotiate a wage above scale. As will be discussed below, the wages above scale are subsumed class payments.

16. Musicians may also receive wages for their subsumed and non-class positions. Indeed these wages may be zero or even negative as will be discussed below. Their regular wages however are always positive by law.

17. Wages for March 3, 2008 through August 31, 2008.

18. The minimum pension benefit paid to each Broadway musician is 5%; however, because of an April 26, 1963, arbitration award to Burton Turkus, the Broadway musicians enjoy pension payments averaging 21–23%.

19. Article IX. "Doubling."

20. When the musicians work overtime, i.e., more than 3 hours per show, two shows on Sunday, or 3 shows on any given day they receive a premium of 50%. I have deemed this payment to be part of the socially necessary wage musicians receive for their fundamental class production of surplus value.

Musicians do indeed require more socially necessary commodities when they work overtime and may have to pay premiums for those commodities. For example, child-care may need to be extended; workers might dine out more often because of the time it takes to prepare a home-cooked meal; and workers might depend on the services of professional house cleaners and lawn maintenance personnel, all of which the musicians' must pay people to perform.

21. This arrangement is obscured by the fact that the Broadway side musicians are legally employees of the theatre owners as discussed in Chapter 2 however, this arrangement is simply an accounting process and one that has been historically in place with no anticipated change in the near future.

22. As will be discussed below, the subsumed class position of surplus value distributor is also a position that the workers hold in a non-exploitative class structure. That is, the goal is for the Broadway musicians themselves to both appropriate and distribute any surplus they produce.

23. This list is not intended to be exhaustive; it is simply a representation of some of the many payments producers must make in order to secure their conditions of existence as capitalists. To be certain, producers must also make payments to stagehands, actors, directors, accountants, lawyers, administrative staff, and advertising personnel, among others.

24. H. Gregg Lewis first brought the 'union wage effect' to the forefront in 1963 in his book, *Unionism and Relative Wages*. Lewis estimated that the impact on wages in a union shop vis-à-vis a non-union shop was approximately 10–15%. Much has been written and debated about 'union wage effects' since then; however, a detailed discussion regarding this issue is peripheral to this book. For example, some authors argue that because workers in a union shop receive higher wages than their nonunion counterparts, that the best, most productive workers tend toward employment where unions exist. On the other hand, other researchers question whether there is a union wage effect at all. For a complete discussion on the union wage effect see Richard Freeman and James Medoff, *What Do Unions Do?* 1984, Chapter 3, "The Union Wage Effect."

25. Article III.G. "Wage Scales."

26. Appendix B, *League Proposals*.

27. Article III.C. "Wage Scales" states "An Associate Conductor shall be employed for all musical shows and be given billing together with the credits on the credits page of the theatre program. The Associate Conductor shall receive thirty percent (30%) additional over and above the appropriate applicable rates set forth herein."

28. The Producer was obliged to pay any one musician the premium at every performance, no matter his/her ability or skill.

29. For intelligibility, I use the term Music Coordinator for the managerial position that is contracted directly by the Producers. The MC assembles and hires an orchestra for the musical show—in other words, he is the labor broker, Marx's parasite, mentioned above. This person is more readily known on Broadway as the "contractor."

On the other hand, the collective bargaining agreement also requires a "designated" or "in-house" "contractor" who must be a playing musician in the orchestra. S/he performs the duties of a personnel manager, i.e., keeping attendance and daily records with regard to the orchestra. Furthermore, the designated contractor routinely acts as an intermediary between the orchestra, the union, and the employers—often taking the responsibilities that a union steward would assume in a conventional union shop arrangement. To complicate matters further, the designated contractor may also be the

MC. For example, Mr. Seymour "Red" Press is the MC, the designated contractor, and also a woodwinds playing musician for the musical "Chicago." Simultaneously, Mr. Press often is the MC for other Broadway productions. He may not, however, be a playing musician in more than one musical at the same time, so this precludes him from being a designated contractor in more than one show concurrently.

30. Refer to the section discussing theatre owners provided in Chapter 2.
31. Of course with the other surplus value producing workers, e.g., the actors.
32. MC John Miller routinely demands that the musicians report to work a half an hour early. No musician will file a grievance over this because of the fear of retaliation. Additionally, as their union representative, I was only given this information because I assured the musicians of confidentiality.
33. Indeed workers who produce no surplus value, for example the concessions clerk, W_1 would be zero. However, because the Broadway musicians produce surplus value, they receive a positive W_1.
34. Broadway musicians individually negotiate any over-scale payments with their employers; Local 802 officials do not take part in this process. Additionally, the musicians do not pay union dues of 3% on over-scale payments, the musicians only pay the 3% dues on the minimum scale wages—this does however, include contracted premiums such as overtime and doubling.
35. In a survey by the Theatre Committee, the Broadway musicians made it clear that over-scale payments were not an issue for negotiations, meaning the status quo was acceptable.
36. Indeed, one of the principal barriers to class transformation might be the notion that communism is somehow 'un-American." This abhorrence of Communism like the type that existed in the former USSR, can undermine the very notion of class transformation. While a complete discussion of union history is beyond the scope of this book, over the past 100 years or so unions made great strides to disassociate themselves with Communists and their radical commentators.
37. Persuading union officials and members will be problematic, given that communism is dismissed as some passé fascist doctrine that was eradicated with the fall of the State "Communism" in the Soviet Bloc (Resnick and Wolff, *Class Theory*).
38. While a communist class process in itself does not necessarily entail democratic hiring and administration procedures, it is my hope that the union through its by-laws and edicts will take transformation a step further and include democratic processes in its endeavors.
39. Many surplus distributions are legally and cultural mandated, therefore, the Broadway musicians would not have complete license in making surplus distributions. These communist surplus distributions, as in any class structure are overdetermined by a countless array of desires and wishes of diverse individuals and/or institutions.
40. If they wish, the musicians could opt to change the wage structure as it was presented above in the section above titled Musicians' Wages Part III.
41. Many of the administrative services that might be necessary to secure communist conditions of existence are already in place. Among other administrative tasks, Local 802 currently provides administrators for health and pension benefits, makes payments to musicians for recording engagements, and provides counseling services to musicians through the Musicians' Assistance Plan (MAP). Additionally, a working musician in every orchestra currently has personnel manager responsibilities for payroll, vacation assignments, and so forth.

42. Currently both the Union Pension fund and the Health Care fund are funded through employer contributions entirely. Musicians cannot individually buy into either fund. Additionally, employers and the union jointly administer both funds. Therefore, either the funds' administration would have to be changed making it possible for the union to make payments on behalf of the Broadway musicians, or some contingency in the contract with the Producers could spell out that the Producers would make payments on behalf of the musicians to these funds. This is but a mere technicality that can be worked out in a variety of ways, not an obstruction to class-transformation, but one of array of possible idiosyncratic nuances Local 802 and the Broadway musicians will need to address.

43. This musician earns a 50% wage premium for these responsibilities.

44. Recall that Broadway musicals are often short-lived, most usually running for less than six months. Consequently, musicians are always thinking about the "next" show, about retaining a job as a Broadway musician.

45. The conductor is a direct employee of the Producer (see Chapter 2 and below).

46. Neither Local 802, its members, nor the League and its members have ever discussed changing this relationship.

47. Broadway musicians that do not hold the position of conductor are considered "side-musicians."

48. One of the goals of this book is to promote democracy and voice among the musicians including conductors through class-transformation. Albeit democracy is not a prerequisite for class-transformation and therefore, a democratically selected conductor is preferred to one that is merely appointed or hired by the Producer.

NOTES TO CHAPTER 5

1. The building trades unions are typically quite ideologically conservative and therefore might reject any class transformation ideas. However, they do present a particular example that is fundamental to this discussion.

2. It may seem counter to union organizing attempts to restrict access to membership; however, it should be noted that many building trades' union workers are unemployed at any particular point in a year. For example, the Local 188 of the Plumbers and Steamfitters union in Fort Wayne, Indiana announced a 30% unemployment rate in November 2005.

3. The apprentice works full-time during the training and education period.

4. According to Leo Ball "the busy day was Wednesday, as Monday was too early for the contractors to have their weekend dates completely organized, and Friday was 'desperation' day, both for contractors with last minute needs, and for the musicians still without [work for] the weekend" (*E-mail*).

5. Club dates include events such as private parties, weddings, and bar mitzvahs.

6. Contractors for club-date offices and leaders were considered 'insiders' and were themselves members of Local 802. An outsider might include an employer looking for an orchestra for a specific event; these employers could therefore only get an entire orchestra through contractors or bandleaders. That is, the contractors and bandleaders formed orchestras and then sold them to an 'employer,' restricting access to musicians from anyone other than themselves.

7. Local 802 has a standard club-date contract that is negotiated between the union and club-date offices, such as Steven Scott Orchestras.

8. Employing a manager would not compromise the musicians' position as a communist appropriator of surplus labor; the manager's wages would simply

be a distribution from communist surplus for his/her subsumed class position as manager.

9. Democratic hiring standards are not essential elements to ensure the communist class process. Indeed, the manager could assign positions as s/he desires and not necessarily solicit voice and participation from the workers. As long as the musicians themselves appropriate and make distribution the surplus labor, the class process remains communist. Nonetheless, in my view democratic administration is the preferred arrangement because I believe it is more egalitarian than other processes.

10. Some of the more established (experienced) conductors currently consult with the music coordinators about which musicians are employed for the show. The consultation, however, depends on the relative power the conductor wields vis-à-vis the music coordinators. The Producers usually give the conductors this power.

11. The Producers currently employ the conductors who are on the Producers' payrolls, not on the theatre owners. It is very probable that the Producers would not yield this position during bargaining with the musicians. This fact, however, does not preclude the proposed communist class arrangement. If the Producers retain the right to choose/hire conductors (who are now represented by Local 802), the union could decide to include the conductor in the hiring process. Conversely, the conductor's voice in the hiring process would not alter the communist arrangement. The conductor's participation in the appropriation and distribution of the surplus labor produced is necessary for the communist class process to remain. As discussed in Chapter 2, conductors in their roles as orchestra leaders are indeed productive workers, and as such, to ensure a communist class process, their participation in the appropriation process is vital.

12. During my more than two years as the Broadway Representative, I made many of these discoveries. Indeed, I filed grievances or discussed the issues with the Producers without ever disclosing that a Broadway musician instigated the investigation.

13. Of course this fee might be set by a collective bargaining agreement between the League and Local 802, which explicitly states the terms of orchestra's price. This would not be much of a change from what is currently in place; however, rather than paying the theatre owners, who in turn pay the musicians, the Producers would now send the payment for the musicians' services directly to Local 802 for distribution. This is the same process the musicians' health and pension benefits.

Bibliography

Abowd, John M. and Henry S. Farber. "Job Queues and the Union Status of Workers." *Industrial and Labor Relations Review* 35.3 (1982): 354–367.

Alpert, Hollis. *Broadway!: 125 Years of Musical Theatre.* New York: Arcade, 1991.

Amann, Robert J. and Ronnie Silverblatt. "High School Students' Views on Unionism." *Labor Studies Journal* 12.3 (1987–1988): 44–60.

American Federation of Labor and Congress of Industrial Workers Organizations (AFL-CIO). *The New American Workplace: A Labor Perspective.* A Report by The AFL-CIO Committee on the Evolution of Work: Washington DC, 1994.

———. "The Union Difference." *AFL-CIO: American's Union Movement.* 26 Jan. 2006, AFL-CIO. 20 Feb 2006 <http://www.aflcio.org/issues/factsstats/index.cfm>.

———. "Common Sense Economics." *AFL-CIO: American's Union Movement.* 20 Apr. 2000, AFL-CIO. 20 Apr. 2000 <http://www.aflcio.org/cse/mod5/situation1.htm>.

———. "Common Sense Economics." *AFL-CIO: American's Union Movement.* 20 Apr. 2000, AFL-CIO. 20 Apr. 2000 <http://www.aflcio.org/cse/mod5/situation2.htm>.

———. "Common Sense Economics." *AFL-CIO: American's Union Movement.* 20 Apr. 2000, AFL-CIO. 20 Apr. 2000 <http://www.aflcio.org/cse/mod5/situation7.htm>.

———. "Unions and the Economy: It's Up to Us," *AFL-CIO: American's Union Movement.* 20 Apr. 2000, AFL-CIO. 20 Apr. 2000 <http://www.aflcio.org/cse/mod6/index.htm>.

———. "Why You Need A Union." *AFL-CIO: American's Union Movement.* 24 Mar. 2002, AFL-CIO. 26 Jan. 2006 <http://www.aflcio.org/joinaunion/why/index.cfm>.

American Federation of Musicians, *Bylaws of the AFM of the United States and Canada*, NY: 1995 n.p.

———. "Collective Bargaining Agreement between The League of American Theatres & Producers, Inc. and the Associated Musicians of Greater New York, Local 802, AFM, AFL-CIO, 1993–1998.

Anderson, P. "The Limits and Possibilities of Trade Union Action." *Trade Unions Under Capitalism.* Ed. T. Clarke and L. Clements. Brighton, UK: Harvester, 1978. 333–350.

Annunziato, Frank. R. "Gramsci's Theory of Trade Unionism." *Rethinking Marxism* 1.2 (1988): 142–164.

———. "Commodity Unionism." *Rethinking Marxism* 3.2 (1990): 8–33.

AOL®Hometown. "Fx Facts and Hazards." 14 Aug. 2005, AOL. 7 Feb. 2006 <http://hometown.aol.com/lungsworking/fxfactshazards.htm>.

Applebaum, Eileen, and Rosemary Batt. *The New American Workplace*. Ithaca, NY: ILR, 1994.

Aronowitz, Stanley. *False Promises: The Shaping of American Working Class Consciousness*. New York: McGraw-Hill, 1973.

Atkins, Richard. "Getting A Broadway Job." *Allegro: Musician's Voice*. CIII. 3 March 2003, Local 802, AFM. 15 Aug. 2005 < http://www.local802afm.org/frames/fs_news.cfm?xPublication=90511721>.

Atkinson, Brooks. *Broadway*. New York: Macmillan, 1990.

Audible Difference. "Musicians-Protecting the Professional Ear." February 7, 2006 <http://www.audible-difference.com/musicians.htm>.

Babin, Angela. "Bring in Da Funk, Leave Out the Noise." *Art Hazard News* 19.4 (1996): 1.

Bacon, David. "Labor Needs a Radical Vision." *Monthly Review* 57.2 (June 2005): 38–45.

Ball, Leo. "Wednesdays at Roseland." *Allegro* (December, 1993): 14.

———. E-mail interview. 16 April 2004.

Barkin, Solomon. *The Decline of the Labor Movement*. Santa Barbara, CA: Center for the Study of Democratic Institutions, 1961.

Baumol, Hilda, and William J. Baumol. *Inflation and the Performing Arts*. New York: New York UP, 1984.

Baumol, William. J., and William G. Bowen. *Performing Arts: The Economic Dilemma*. MA: MIT, 1966.

Beirne, Joseph A. *Challenge to Labor: New Roles for American Trade Unions*. NJ: Prentice-Hall, 1969.

Bell, Marty. *Broadway Stories: A Backstage Journey Through Musical Theatre*. New York: Broadway Cares/Equity Fights AIDS, 1993.

Benson, Susan Porter. "Class Consciousness and Solidarity: Perspectives East and West." *Reviews In American History* 8.2 (1980): 251–257.

Bernard, Elaine. *Why Unions Matter*. NJ: New Party Paper 4, Open Magazine, Pamphlet Series, 1996.

Bernheim, Alfred L., and Sara Harding. *The Business of the Theatre: An Economic History of the American Theatre, 1730–1932*. New York: Benjamin Blom; Actors' Equity Association, 1932.

Bernstein, Aaron. "Why America Needs Unions, But Not The Kind It Has Now." *Business Week* 23 (May 1994): 70–82.

Bitterman, Brooks. "Geography and Workers' Struggles: The Strategic Use of Place and Space by Labor and Capital." Diss. Clark, 1996.

Blom, Raimo. "The Relevance of Class Theory." *Acta Sociologica* 283 (1985): 171–192.

Bognanno, Mario F., and Morris M. Kleiner. *Labor Market Institutions and The Future Role of Unions*. Cambridge, MA: Blackwell, 1992.

Booth, Douglas E. "Collective Action, Marx's Class Theory, and the Union Movement." *Journal of Economic Issues* 121 (1978): 163–185.

Bordman, Gerald. *American Musical Revue*. New York: Oxford UP, 1985.

Bramel, Dana, and Clemencia Ortiz. "Tomorrow's Workers and Today's Unions: A Survey of High School Students." *Labor Studies Journal* 11.3 (1987–1988): 28–43.

"Broadway Season Statistics." Live Broadway.com. 3 June 2005, League of American Theatres and Producers. 20 Feb. 2006 <http://www.livebroadway.com/bwaystats.html>.

Brody, David. *The American Labor Movement*. New York: Harper & Row, 1971.

———. *Workers in Industrial America: Essays on the Twentieth Century Struggle*. UK: Oxford UP, 1993.

Bronfenbrenner, Kate, et al. *Organizing to Win.* Ithaca, New York: ILR Press, 1998.

Carré, Francoise J., Virginia Durivage, and Chris Tilly. "Representing the Part-Time and Contingent Workforce: Challenges for Unions and Public Policy" Sheldon Friedman, Richard W. Hurd, Rudolph Oswald and Ronald Seeber. Eds. *Restoring the Promise of American Law.* Ithaca, NY: Cornell UP; Industrial and Labor Relations Press, 1994.

Church, Joseph. "Analysis of Creative Process in the Composition of a New Musical Work: 'Les Fables.'" Diss. New York University, 1996.

Clawson, Dan, Karen Johnson, and John Schall. "Fighting Union Busting in the 80's." *Radical America* 16 (1983): 44–62.

CNN Interactive. "Workers Say Sickness Showed Up Early." *Showbiz News.* 15 Dec. 1998, CNN.com. 21 Feb. 2006 <http://cgi.cnn.com/SHOWBIZ/9801/01/disney.woes/index2.html?>.

Cohan, George Michael. *Twenty Years on Broadway and the Years it Took to Get There; The True Story of A Trouper's Life from the Cradle to the "Closed Shop."* New York and London: Harper & Brothers, 1925.

Cohen-Stratyner, B., and B. Kueppers, eds. *Preserving America's Performing Arts: Papers from the Conference on Preservation Management for Performing Arts Collection, April 28-May 1, 1982.* Washington D. C. and New York: Theatre Library Association, 1985.

Cottle, Rex L., Hugh H. Macaulay, and T. Bruce Yandle. "Codetermination: Union Style." *Journal of Labor Research* 4.2 (1983): 125–135.

Culf, Nicola. *Musicians' Injuries: a Guide to their Understanding and Prevention.* UK: Parapress, 1998.

Cullenberg, Stephen. "Socialism's Burden: Toward a 'Thin' Definition of Socialism." *Rethinking Marxism* 5.2 (Summer 1992): 64–83.

Cutcher-Gershenfeld, Joel. "Labor-Management Cooperation in American Communities: What's in it for the Unions?" *The Annals* 473 (1984): 76–87.

Davis, Christopher. *The Producer.* New York: Harper & Row, 1972.

Davis, Mike, and Michael Sprinkler, eds. *Reshaping The US Left: Popular Struggles In The 1980's.* New York: Verso, 1988.

Demartino, George. "Trade-Union Isolation and the Catechism of the Left." *Rethinking Marxism* 4.3 (1991): 29–51.

Dickman, Howard. *Industrial Democracy in America.* LaSalle, IL: Open Court, 1987.

Doucouliagos, Chris. "Worker Participation and Productivity in Labor-Managed and Participatory Capitalist Firms: A Meta-Analysis." *Industrial and Labor Relations Review* 49.1 (1995): 58–77.

Economic Policy Institute. "Rising Inflation Due to Profit Margins and Energy, Not Labor Costs." *Economic Snapshots* 26 May 2004, EPI. 21 Feb. 2006 <http://www.epinet.org/printer.cfm?id=1800&content_type=1&nice_name=webfeatures_snapshots_05262004>.

Edwards, Richard and Michael Podgursky. "The Unraveling Accord: American Unions in Crisis." *Unions in Crisis and Beyond: Perspectives from Six Countries.* Ed. Richard Edwards, Paolo Garonna, and Franz Tödtling. Dover, MA: Auburn House, 1986: 14–60.

Edwards, Richard, Paolo Garonna, and Franz Tödtling. *Unions in Crisis and Beyond: Perspectives from Six Countries.* Dover, MA: Auburn House, 1986.

Ellerman, David. *The Democratic Worker-Owned Firm.* Boston, MA: Unwin Hyman, 1990.

Elsila, Mikael. "Labor Board Rules That Apollo Band Can Form Union." *Allegro* C.12 December 2000, Local 802, AFM. 21 Feb. 2006 <http://www.local802afm.org/frames/fs_news.cfm?xPublication=90511721>.

Engels, Fredrick. "The Principles of Communism." *Selected Works* (1969): 81–97.

"Enlightenment Quotations." *Thomas Jefferson.* April 2002, Futurehealth.org. 21 Feb. 2006 <www.futurehealth.org/enlightenment_quotations.htm>.

Eustis, Morton. *B'way, Inc.!: The Theatre as a Business.* New York: Dodd Mead, 1934.

Ewen, David. *The Story of America's Musical Theater.* Philadelphia: Chilton, 1961.

Fantasia, Rick, Dan Clawson, and Gregory Graham. "A Critical View of Worker Participation in American Industry." *Work and Occupations* (Nov. 1988): 468–488.

Farber, Donald C. *Producing On Broadway.* New York: DBS, 1969.

———. *Producing Theatre: A Comprehensive Legal and Business Guide.* New York: Limelight, 1997.

Farber, Henry. "The Decline of Unionization in the United States: What Can Be Learned from Recent Experience?" *Journal of Labor Economics* 8.1 (1990): S75-S105.

Ferguson, William D. "Declining Union Bargaining Power and the Rising Wage-Productivity Gap in the U.S. Economy Since the Late 1970's." Diss. University of Massachusetts, Amherst, MA, 1989.

Forbes, Ian, and John Street. "Individual Transitions to Socialism." *Theory, Culture and Society* 3.1 (1986): 17–32.

Fraad, Harriet, Stephen Resnick and Richard Wolff. *Bring it All Back Home: Class, Gender & Power in the Modern Household.* London: Pluto, 1994.

Freeman, Richard B. "The Effect of the Union Wage Differential on Management Opposition and Union Organizing Success." *American Economic Review* (May 1986): 92–96.

Freeman, Richard B., and James L. Medoff. *What Do Unions Do?* New York: Basic, 1984.

Freeman, Richard B., and Joel Rogers. "Who Speaks For Us? Employee Representation in a Non-Union Labor Market." *Employee Representation: Alternatives and Future Directions.* Ed. Bruce. E. Kaufman and Morris M. Kleiner. Madison, WI: Industrial Relations Research Assn., 1993. 13–80.

Freeman, Richard B., and Morris M. Kleiner. "Employer Behavior in the Face of Union Organizing Drives." *Industrial and Labor Relations Review* 43.4 (1990): 351–365.

Fields, Armond, and L. Marc Fields. *From The Bowery to Broadway: Lew Fields and The Roots of American Popular Theatre.* New York: Oxford UP, 1993.

Flinn, Denny Martin. *Musical! A Grand Tour: The Rise, Glory, and Fall of an American Institution.* New York: Prentice Hall International, 1997.

Friedman, Gerald. "The Decline of the American Labor Movement: Explanations and Implications for United States Industrial Relations." Political Economy Seminar. University of Massachusetts, Amherst, MA. 1998, n.p.

Frommer, Myrna Katz, and Harvey F. Frommer. *It Happened on Broadway: An Oral History of the Great White Way.* New York: Harcourt Brace, 1998.

Fusco, Victor. "Carpal Tunnel Syndrome: Causes and Treatments." *Allegro* C.4 April 2000, Local 802, AFM. 21 Feb. 2006 <http://www.local802afm.org/frames/fs_news.cfm?xPublication=90511721>.

Galenson, Walter. *The American Labor Movement, 1955–1995.* Westport, CN: Greenwood, 1996.

Gaspasin Fernando E., and Michael D. Yates, "Labor Movements: Is There Hope?" *Monthly Review* 57.2 (2005): 3–12.

Gene Levine Associates. "You Can't Lose an Election You Don't Have." *Complete Union Avoidance Manual.* November 2000, Genelevine.com. 20 Feb. 2006. <http://www.genelevine.com/mnualunionavoid.htm>.

Gibson-Graham, J. K. "Waiting For The Revolution, Or How to Smash Capitalism While Working At Home In Your Spare Time." *Rethinking Marxism* 6.2 (1993): 10–24.

———. *The End of Capitalism (As We Knew It)*. Cambridge, MA: Blackwell, 1996.

Gibson-Graham, J. K., S. A., Resnick, and R. D. Wolff. *Class and Its Others*. Minneapolis: U of Minnesota P, 2000.

Gordon, David, Richard Edwards, and Michael Reich. *Segmented Work, Divided Workers*. UK: Cambridge UP, 1982.

Gramsci, Antonio. "Unions and Councils" *Selections From Political Writings (1921–1926)*. Ed. and Trans. Quintin Hoare. London: Lawrence and Wishart, 1978. 20–22.

———. "Worker' Control" *Selections From Political Writings (1921–1926)*. Ed. and Trans. Quintin Hoare. London: Lawrence and Wishart, 1978. 10–11.

———. "Once Again on The Organic Capacities of the Working Class" *Selections From Political Writings (1921–1926)*. Ed. and Trans. Quintin Hoare. London: Lawrence and Wishart, 1978. 417–421.

———. "The Modern Prince" *Selections from the Prison Notebooks*. Ed. and Trans. Quintin Hoare and Geoffrey Nowell Smith. London: Lawrence and Wishart, 1971.

Green, Hardy. *On Strike at Hormel: The Struggle for a Democratic Labor Movement*. Philadelphia: Temple UP, 1990.

Grenier, Guillermo J. *Inhuman Relations: Quality Circles and Anti-Unionism in American Industry*. Philadelphia: Temple UP, 1988.

Griffin, Larry J., Michael E. Wallace, and Beth A. Rubin. "Capitalist Resistance to the Organization of Labor Before The New Deal: Why? How? Success?" *American Sociological Review* 51 (1986): 147–167.

Griffith, Barbara S. *The Crisis of American Labor: Operation Dixie and the Defeat of the CIO*. Philadelphia: Temple UP, 1988.

Grossinger, K. "Can Strikes Still Be Won?" *Social Policy* Spring (1989): 4–12.

Hall, R. R., D. C. Thorns, and W.E. Willmott. "Community, Class, and Kinship—Bases for Collective Action Within Localities." *Society and Space* 2 (1984): 201–215.

Hanagan, Michael, and Charles Stephenson, eds. *Confrontation, Class Consciousness, and the Labor Process: Studies In Proletarian Class Formation*. New York: Greenwood, 1986.

Hansmann, Henry. "When Does Worker Ownership Work? ESOPS, Law Firms, Codetermination, and Economic Democracy" *Yale Law Journal* 99.8 (1990): 1749–1816.

Harris, Andrew Bennett. *Broadway Theatre*. NY: Routledge, 1994.

Hart-Landsberg, Martin, and Jerry Lembcke. "Class Struggle and Economic Transformation." *Journal of Radical Political Economics* 16.4 (1984): 14–31.

Henderson, Mary C. *The City and The Theatre: New York Playhouses From Bowling Green to Times Square*. Clifton, NJ: James T. White, 1973.

Herding, Richard. "Job Control and Union Structure" *Trade Unions Under Capitalism*. Ed. T. Clarke and L. Clements. Brighton, UK: Harvester, 1978. 260–287.

Hillard, Michael, and Richard McIntyre. "The Crises of Industrial Relations as an Academic Discipline in the United States" *Historical Studies In Industrial Relations* 7 (Spring 1999): 75–98.

Hirschman, Albert O. *Exit, Voice, and Loyalty*. MA: Harvard UP, 1970.

Hodgson, Geoffrey M., and Derek C. Jones. "Codetermination: A Partial Review of Theory and Evidence." *Annals of Public and Co-Operative Economy*, 60.3 (1989): 329–340.

Hotch, Janet. "Theories and Practices of Self-Employment: Prospects for the Labor Movement." Master of Science Thesis. LLRC-University of Massachusetts, 1994.

Houghton, Norris. *Entrances & Exits: A Life in and out of the Theatre.* New York: Limelight, 1991.

Ilson, Carol. *Harold Prince: From Pajama Game to Phantom of the Opera and Beyond.* New York: Limelight, 1992.

Jackman, Mary R. and Robert W. Jackman. *Class Awareness In The United States.* Berkeley: U of P, 1983.

Jenson, Jane and Rianne Mahon, eds. *The Challenge of Restructuring: North American Labor Movements Respond.* Philadelphia: Temple UP, 1993.

Kaufman, Bruce E. "The Determinants of Strikes In The United States, 1900–1977." *Industrial and Labor Relations Review* 35.4 (1982): 473–490.

Kerr, Walter. *The Theater In Spite of Itself.* New York: Simon and Schuster, 1963.

———. *Journey to The Center of The Theater.* New York: Knopf, 1979.

Kessler-Harris, Alice. "Trade Unions Mirror Society In Conflict Between Collectivism and Individualism." *Monthly Labor Review* (August 1987): 32–36.

Kislan, Richard. *The Musical: A Look At The American Musical Theater.* New Jersey: Prentice-Hall, 1980.

Kistler, Alan. "Union Organizing: New Challenges and Prospects." *The Annals* 473 (1984): 96–107.

Kochan, Thomas A. "How American Workers View Labor Unions." *Monthly Labor Review* (April 1979): 23–31.

Kornbluh, Hy. "Work Place Democracy and Quality of Work Life: Problems and Prospects." *The Annals* 473 (1984): 88–95.

Labor Research Association. "U.S. Union Membership: 1948–2004." *LRAonline.org.* Apr. 2005, LRA. 26 Jan. 2006 <http://www.lraonline.org/charts.php?id=29>.

———. "Union Membership: Private Sector: 1948–2004." *LRAonline.org.* Apr. 2005, LRA. 26 Jan. 2006 <http://www.laborresearch.org/charts.php?id=53>.

———. "Unions Have the Resources for Growth in Major Metropolitan Areas." *LRAonline.org.* 9 Sept. 2001, LRA. 26 Jan. 2006 <http://www.laborresearch.org/page_src.php?id=12&src=Metro>.

Lapides, Kenneth. *Marx and Engels On The Trade Unions.* New York: Praeger, 1987.

Langley, Stephen. *Theatre Management and Production In America.* New York: Drama Book, 1990.

Lash, Scott and John Urry. "The New Marxism of Collective Action: A Critical Analysis." *Sociology* 18.1 (1984): 33–50.

Laufe, Abe. *Broadway's Great Musicals.* New York: Funk & Wagnalls, 1969.

League of American Theatres and Producers, Inc. and the Alliance for the Arts, *Broadway's Economic Contribution to New York City.* 2000–2001.

League of American Theatres and Producers, Inc., and the Associated Musicians of Greater New York, Local 802, AFM, AFL-CIO. *Collective Bargaining Agreements,* 1990,1993,1998, 2003.

———. *Memorandum of Agreement,* 2003.

Lee, Joseph Shing. "An Economic Theory of Union Growth." Diss. University of Massachusetts, Amherst, MA, 1973.

Leggett, John C. *Class, Race, and Labor: Working-Class Consciousness in Detroit.* Oxford, England: Oxford UP, 1968.

Leiter, Samuel L. *Ten Season: New York Theatre in the Seventies.* New York: Greenwood, 1986.

Lembcke, Jerry. *Capitalist Development and Class Capacities: Marxist Theory and Union Organization.* New York: Greenwood, 1988.

Lennon, David. "Local 802 and League Evaluate Health and Safety 'Prototypes.'" *Allegro* CII.7/8 July 2002, Local 802, AFM. 21 Feb.2006 <http://www. local802afm.org/frames/fs_news.cfm?xPublication=90511721>.
———. "The Issue." Local 802, AFM. 20 January 2006 <http://www.savelive-broadway.com/issue.html?e_e=43fe326d737f373e_95103>.
Levison, Andrew. *The Working-Class Majority*. New York: Coward, McCann, and Geoghegan, 1974.
Levitan, Sar A., and Clifford M.Johnson. "The Changing Work Place." *The Annals* 473 (1984): 116–127.
Lindblom, Charles E. *Unions and Capitalism*. New Haven, CN: Yale UP, 1949.
Lipset, Seymour Martin. *American Exceptionalism?: A Double-Edged Sword.* New York: Norton, 1979.
Loney, Glenn, ed. *Musical Theatre In America*. Greenwood,1984.
Lynd, Alice, and Staughton Lynd, eds. *Rank and File: Personal Histories By Working-Class Organizers*. Princeton, NJ: Princeton UP, 1981.
Lynd, Staughton. *Solidarity Unionism: Rebuilding The Labor Movement From Below*. Chicago: Charles H. Kerr, 1992.
———. "Marx, The Present Crisis and the Future of Labour." *The Socialist Register* (1986): 436–454.
Mantsios, Gregory. *A New Labor Movement For The New Century*. New York: Monthly Review Press, 1998.
Maranto, Cheryl L. "Employee Participation: An Evaluation of Labor Policy Alternatives." *Contemporary Economic Policy* 12.4 (1994): 57–66.
Martin, Ron, Peter Sunley, and Jane Wills. "Unions and The Politics of Deindustrialization: Some Comments On How Geography Complicates Class Analysis" *Antipode* 26.1 (1994): 59–76.
Marx, Karl. *Wage-Labour and Capital*. New York: International, 1997.
———. *Value, Price, and Profit*. Chicago: Charles H. Kerr, 1997.
———. *Theories of Surplus Value: Part I, II, III*. Moscow: Progress, 1975.
———. *Capital, Volume 1*. UK: Penguin Classics, 1976.
———. *Capital, Volume 2*. UK: Penguin Classics, 1978.
———. *Capital, Volume 3*. UK: Penguin Classics, 1981.
Masters, Marick F. *Unions At The Crossroads: Strategic Membership, Financial, and Political Perspectives*. Westport, CT: Quorum, 1997.
Mates, Julian. *America's Musical Stage: Two Hundred Years of Musical Theatre.* CT: Greenwood. 1985.
Matza, David, and David Wellman. "The Ordeal of Consciousness" *Theory and Society* 9 (1980): 1–27.
McCain, Roger A. "Transaction Costs, Labor Management, and Codetermination." *Advances In The Economic Analysis of Participatory and Labor-Managed Firms* 4 (1992): 205–222.
McCammon, Holly J. "Legal Limits On Labor Militancy: U.S. Labor Law and The Right to Strike Since The New Deal." *Social Problems* 37.2 (1990): 206–229.
McDermott, John. *The Crisis In The Working Class and Some Arguments For A New Labor Movement*. Boston, MA: South End, 1990.
McDermott, John. "Free Enterprise and Socialized Labor." *Science and Society* 55.4 (1991): 388–416.
McDonald, Charles. "U.S. Union Membership in Future Decades: A Trade Unionist's Perspective." *Industrial Relations* 31.1 (Winter 1992): 13–30.
McGovern, Dennis, and Deborah Grace Winer. *Sing Out, Louise!* New York: Schrimer, 1993.
McKinley, Jesse. "On Stage and Off." *New York Times* 30 March 2001: E2.

———. "Having Reshaped Broadway, Disney Readies a Second Act." *New York Times* 29 November 2003 <http://www.nytimes.com/2003/11/29/arts/theater/29DISN.html?th=&pagewanted=print&position=>.

McNall, Scott. G., Rhonda F. Levine, and Rick Fantasia. *Bringing Class Back In: Contemporary and Historical Perspectives*. Boulder, CO: Westview, 1991.

McNamara, Brooks. *The Shuberts of Broadway*. New York: Oxford UP, 1990.

Miller, John, Jill Dell'Abate and Neil Balm. "Meet the Contractors." *Allegro* CV.1 January 2005, Local 802, AFM. 21 Feb. 2006 <http://www.local802afm.org/frames/fs_news.cfm?xPublication=90511721>.

Mishel, Lawrence, Jared Bernstein, and John Schmitt. *The State of Working America: 1998–1999*. Economic Policy Institute, ILR. 1999.

Moberly, Robert B. "Worker Participation after *Electromation* and *Du Pont*." *Restoring The Promise of American Labor Law*. Ed. Sheldon Friedman, et. al. Ithaca, NY: ILR, 1994: 147–160.

Moline, Jacqueline. "Preliminary Report-Local 802, American Federation of Musicians." 18 November 1996.

Moore, Thomas Gale. *The Economics of The American Theater*. Durham, NC: Duke UP, 1968.

Moore, William J., and Robert J. Newman. "The Effects of Right-to-Work Laws: A Review of The Literature." *Industrial and Labor Relations Review* 38.4 (1985): 571–585.

Mordden, Ethan. *Better Foot Forward: The History of American Musical Theatre*. New York: Grossman, 1976.

———. *Broadway Babies: The People Who Made The American Musical*. New York: Oxford UP, 1983.

———. *Coming Up Roses: The Broadway Musical In The 1950s*. New York: Oxford UP, 1998.

Moriarity, William. "The History of Broadway Theatre Minimums: President's Report." *Allegro* CII.5 May 2002, Local 802, AFM. 21 Feb. 2006 <http://www.local802afm.org/frames/fs_news.cfm?xPublication=90511721>.

———. "Broadway's Future Depends on You, President's Report." *Allegro* CIII.5 May, 2003, Local 802, AFM. 21 Feb. 2006 <http://www.local802afm.org/frames/fs_article.cfm?xEntry=81621809>.

———. Personal Interview. 14 March 2003. New York.

Moses, John A. *Trade Union Theory From Marx to Walesa*. New York: St. Martin's, 1990.

National Endowment For The Arts. Research Division. *Conditions and Needs of the Professional American Theatre*. Washington : NEA; [New York Distributed By Publishing Center For Cultural Resources], 1981. National Endowment For The Arts Research Division Report; 11.

Navarro, Vicente. "Social Movements and Class Politics in the US." *The Socialist Register* (1988): 425–447.

Nuti, Domenico Mario. "Codetermination, Profit Sharing, and Full Employment" *Advances In The Economic Analysis of Participatory and Labor-Managed Firms* 3 (1988): 169–183.

Ollman, Bertell. "How to Study Class Consciousness, and Why We Should." *The Insurgent Sociologist* 14 (1987): 57–96.

Oswald, R. "New Directions For American Unionism." *The Annals* 473 (1984): 141–148.

Parker, M., and J. Slaughter. *Choosing Sides: Unions and The Team Concept*. Boston: South End, 1988.

Peiken, Matt. "A Real Pain." *St. Paul Pioneer Press* October 28, 2002 <http://www.mattpeiken.com/Clips/Music/horvath.htm>.

Pereira, John W. *Opening Nights: 25 Years of The Manhattan Theatre Club.* New York: Peter Lang, 1996.

Perlman, Selig. *A History of Trade Unionism in the United States.* New York: Augustus M. Kelly, 1950.

———. *The Theory of the Labor Movement.* New York: Augustus M. Kelly, 1970.

Peterson, Richard B., Thomas W. Lee, and Barbara Finnegan. "Strategies and Tactics in Union Organizing Campaigns." *Industrial Relations* 32.2 (Spring 1992): 370–381.

Pill, Michael. "Labor Law and Economics: Case Study of the National Labor Relations Act." Diss. University of Massachusetts, Amherst, MA. 1983.

Poggi, Jack. *Theater In America: The Impact of Economic Forces, 1870–1967.* Ithaca, NY: Cornell UP, 1968.

Pogrebin, Robin. "2 Chouses Out of Sync." *New York Times* (March 3, 2003): B1.

Porter, Susan L. *With An Air Debonair: Musical Theatre In America, 1785–1815.* Washington, DC: Smithsonian Institution, 1991.

Press, Seymour 'Red.' Personal Interview. 4 May 2003. Forest Hills, NY.

———. E-mail interview. 3 Dec. 2004.

Rachleff, Peter. *Hard-Pressed In The Heartland: The Hormel Strike and The Future of The Labor Movement.* Boston: South End, 1993.

Resnick, Stephen. A. and Richard D. Wolff. *Knowledge and Class: A Marxian Critique of Political Economy.* IL: U of Chicago P, 1987.

Resnick, Stephen. A. and Richard D. Wolff. *Class Theory and History: Capitalism and Communism in the U.S.S.R.* . New York: Routledge, 2002.

Robinson, J. Gregg. "American Unions In Decline: Problems and Prospects." *Critical Sociology* 15.1 (1988): 33–56.

Rockefeller Brothers Fund. *The Performing Arts: Problems and Prospects; Rockefeller Panel Report On The Future of Theatre, Dance, Music In America.* New York: McGraw-Hill, 1965.

Rogers, Joel. "A Strategy for Labor." *Industrial Relations* 34.3 (July 1995): 367–381.

Roomer, John E. "Neoclassicism, Marxism, and Collective Action." *Journal of Economic Issues* 12.1 (1978): 147–161.

Rose, Frank. *The Agency and The Hidden History of Show.* New York: Harper Business, 1995.

Rose, Joseph B., and Gary N. Chaison. "Linking Union Density and Union Effectiveness: The North American Experience." *Industrial Relations* 35.1 (January 1996): 78–103.

Rosenberg, Bernard and Ernest Harburg. *The Broadway Musical: Collaboration in Commerce and Art.* New York: New York UP, 1993.

Ross, Robert J. S., and Kent C. Trachte. *Global Capitalism: The New Leviathan.* Albany, NY: State University of New York, 1990.

Rothstein, Lawrence. "Industrial Justice Meets Industrial Democracy: Liberty of Expression at the Workplace in the U.S. and France." *Labor Studies Journal* (Fall 1988): 18–39.

Schrecker, Ellen. "McCarthyism and Organized Labor." *Working USA* 3.5 (2000): 93–101.

Simon, John Ivan. *Uneasy Stages: A Chronicle of The New York Theater, 1963–1973.* New York: Random House, 1975.

Skinner, Joseph. "Free Speech and The Market Economy." *Monthly Review* (November 1991): 28–32.

Slaughter, Jane. *Concessions and How to Beat Them.* Detroit: Labor Education and Research Project, 1983.

———. "What Went Wrong In Detroit? Business-As-Usual Unionism Lost The Newspaper Strike." *Labor Notes* Feb. 2001, LaborNotes.org. 21 Feb. 2006 <http://labornotes.org/archives/2001/0201/0201b.html>.

Sponberg, Arvid F. *Broadway Talks: What Professionals Think About Commercial Theater in America.* New York: Greenwood, 1991.

St. Antoine, Theodore J. "Changing Concepts of Worker Rights In The Work Place." *The Annals* 473 (1984): 108–115.

Stefanova-Peteva, Kalilna. *Who Calls The Shots On The New York Stages.* Langhorne, PA: Harwood Academic, 1993.

Stormes, Jim. "The Poor In The United States: A Class-Analytic Approach." *Rethinking Marxism* 1.2 (1988): 76–102.

Svejnar, Jan. "Relative Wage Effects of Unions, Dictatorship and Codetermination: Econometric Evidence From Germany." *Review of Economics and Statistics* 63.2 (1981): 188–197.

Swain, Joseph Peter. *The Broadway Musical: A Critical and Musical Survey.* NY: Oxford UP, 1990.

Taplin, Ian. M. "The Contradictions of Business Unionism and The Decline of Organized Labour." *Economic and Industrial Democracy* 11 (1990): 249–278.

Task Force On Performing Arts Centers. *Bricks, Mortar and The Performing Arts; Report. Background Paper.* New York: Twentieth Century Fund, 1970.

Teschke, Kay, Yat Chow, Michael Brauer, Chris van Netten, Sunil Varughese, and Susan Kennedy. "Atmospheric Effects in the Entertainment Industry: Constituents, Exposures, and Health Effects." *School of Occupational and Environmental Hygiene, University of British Columbia.* 2003, University of British Columbia. 21 Feb. 2006 <http://www.shape.bc.ca/resources/pdf/summary.pdf>.

"Thirteen Broadway Unions and Guilds Form Industry-Wide Coalition: Cobug Eyes Public Policy and Collective Bargaining to Promote Broadway." *Theatre News.* 13 January 2003. Actors' Equity Association. 17 April 2003 <http://www.actorsequity.org/TheatreNews/cobug_01–13–2003.html>.

Tomlins, Christopher L. *The State and The Unions: Labor Relations, Law, and The Organized Labor Movement In America, 1880–1960.* Cambridge, MA: Cambridge UP, 1985.

Tormey, Steve. "Hello, 'Team Concept' Goodbye, 'Quality Circles.'" 2 July 2008, http://quadrant4.org/teamunion.html

Trotsky Leon. "Marxism and Trade Unionism." *Trade Unions Under Capitalism.* Ed. T. Clarke and L. Clements. Brighton, UK: Harvester, 1978: 77–92.

Turnbull, Peter. J. "The Economic Theory of Trade Union Behavior: A Critique." *British Journal of Industrial Relations* 26.1 (1988): 99–118.

Ulman, Lloyd. *The Rise of The National Trade Union: The Development and Significance of Its Structure, Governing Institutions, and Economic Policies.* Cambridge, MA: Harvard UP, 1955.

United States. Committee on Labor and Human Resources United States Senate, Subcommittee on Labor. *Performing Arts Labor Relations Amendments,* 100th Congress, First Session. S. 1346. Washington DC: GPO, 1998.

———. Board of Governors of the Federal Reserve System. "Flow of Funds Accounts of the United States," 1995–2000 and 1965–1974, US Government. 20 Feb. 2006 <http://www.census.gov/population/estimates/nation/popclockest.txt>.

———. Bureau of Labor Statistics. "Union Members Summary." 2004, US Government. 20 Feb. 2006 <http://stats.bls.gov/news.release/union2.nr0.htm>.

———. Department of Labor, Occupational Safety and Health Administration. "Noise Control: A Guide for Workers and Employers." 1980. GPO.

―――. Department of Labor, Occupational Safety and Health Administration. "Occupational Noise Exposure." 2004. US Government. 7 February 2006 <http://www.osha.gov/pls/oshaweb/owadisp.show_document?p_table=STANDARDS&p_id=9735>.

University of Aukland. "Musicians Hearing Loss and Hearing Protection." *Medical and Health Sciences*. 2006. University of Aukland, 21 Feb. 2006 <http://www.health.auckland.ac.nz/audiology/musicians.html>.

Vallas, Stephen P. "White-Collar Proletarians? The Structure of Clerical Work and Levels of Class Consciousness." *The Sociological Quarterly* 28.4 (1987): 523–540.

Vanneman, Richard, and Lynn Weber Cannon. *The American Perception of Class*. Philadelphia: Temple UP, 1987.

Vogel, Harold L. *Entertainment Industry Economics: A Guide for Financial Analysis*. Cambridge, NY: Cambridge UP, 1986.

Walker, Dick. "What's Left to Do?" *Antipode* 21.2 (1989): 133–165.

Weil, David. *Turning the Tide: Strategic Planning for Labor Unions*. New York: Lexington, 1994.

Weiler, Paul C. *Governing the Workplace: The Future of Labor and Employment Law*. Cambridge, MA: Harvard UP, 1990.

Weiner, Ross. "The Political Economy of Organized Baseball: Analysis of a Unique Industry." Diss. University of Massachusetts, Amherst, MA, 1999.

―――. Weiner, Ross D. "Power Hitters Strike Out: New Perspectives on Baseball and Slavery." *Rethinking Marxism* 15.1 (January 2003): 33–48.

Whyte, William Foote, and Joseph R. Blasi. "Employee Ownership and the Future of Unions." *The Annals* 473 (1984): 128–140.

Wilentz, Sean. "Against Exceptionalism: Class Consciousness and the American Labor Movement, 1790–1920." *International Labor and Working Class History* 26 (1984): 1–24.

Winant, Howard. "Postmodern Racial Politics In The United States: Difference and Inequality." *Socialist Review* (1989): 121–147.

Wolff, Richard, "Marxism and Democracy." *Rethinking Marxism* 12.1 (Spring 2000): 112–122.

Wood, Ellen Meiksins. "Marxism Without Class Struggle?" *The Socialist Register* (1983): 239–271.

Yates, Michael. D. *Why Unions Matter*. New York: Monthly Review Press, 1998.

Young, David. *How to Direct A Musical: Broadway—Your Way!* New York: Routledge, 1995.

Zinn, Howard, Dana Frank, and Robin D.G. Kelley. *Three Strikes: Miners, Musicians, Salesgirls, and the Fighting Spirit of Labor's Last Century*. Boston. Beacon, 2001.

Zipp, John F. "Plant Closings and the Conflict Between Capital and Labor." *Research In Social Movements, Conflict, and Change* 6 (1984): 225–248.

―――. Paul Luebke, and Richard Landerman. "The Social Bases of Support For Workplace Democracy" *Sociological Perspectives* 27.4 (1984): 395–425.

Zwerdling, Daniel. *Democracy At Work*. Washington, DC: Association of Self-Management, 1978.

Index

Page numbers in *italics* denotes a table

For Product Safety Concerns and Information please contact our EU
representative GPSR@taylorandfrancis.com
Taylor & Francis Verlag GmbH, Kaufingerstraße 24, 80331 München, Germany

www.ingramcontent.com/pod-product-compliance
Ingram Content Group UK Ltd.
Pitfield, Milton Keynes, MK11 3LW, UK
UKHW020945180425
457613UK00019B/522